By the
Grace
of the
Game

By the Grace of the Game

The Holocaust,
a Basketball Legacy,
and an Unprecedented
American Dream

Dan Grunfeld

TRIUMPH
B O O K S

The Library of Congress has catalogued the hardcover edition as follows:

Names: Grunfeld, Dan, author.
Title: By the grace of the game: the Holocaust, a basketball legacy, and the American dream / Dan Grunfeld.
Description: Chicago, Illinois: Triumph Books, | Summary: "This book details a family's unique story from escaping the Holocaust to landing in America to playing in the NBA"—Provided by publisher.
Identifiers: LCCN 2021019293 (print) | LCCN 2021019294 (ebook) | ISBN 9781629379227 (hardcover) | ISBN 9781641257008 (epub) Subjects: LCSH: Grunfeld, Dan—Family. | Grunfeld, Dan—Childhood and youth. | Basketball players—United States—Biography. | National Basketball Association. | Children of Holocaust survivors—United States—Biography. | Holocaust, Jewish (1939–1945)—Romania—Personal narratives.
Classification: LCC E184.37.G775 A3 2021 (print) | LCC E184.37.G775 (ebook) | DDC 796.323092 [B]—dc23
LC record available at https://lccn.loc.gov/2021019293
LC ebook record available at https://lccn.loc.gov/2021019294

This book is available in quantity at special discounts for your group or organization. For further information, contact:
Triumph Books LLC
814 North Franklin Street
Chicago, Illinois 60610
(312) 337-0747
www.triumphbooks.com

Printed in U.S.A.

ISBN: 978-1-63727-097-4

Design by Sue Knopf

Photos courtesy of Grunfeld family unless otherwise indicated

For Mom, Bec, and Sam

contents

foreword

I've been a student of the Holocaust ever since I saw *Schindler's List* in 1993, when I was just a young college basketball player at UConn. The movie had a profound effect on me. It wasn't because I saw Germans killing Jews; it was because I saw people killing people. I was raised to believe that all human beings should be treated with dignity and respect, regardless of their race, ethnicity, or religion. I was shaken by the knowledge that six million Jews and millions more were murdered by their fellow man. From that day on, I felt an obligation to educate myself on what humanity was capable of. I read books about the Holocaust and watched documentaries. I asked questions. I did my research.

In 1998, as an NBA player for the Milwaukee Bucks, I made my first visit to the U.S. Holocaust Memorial Museum in Washington, D.C. I'll never forget entering a room at the museum filled to the ceiling with pictures of Jews from a town in Poland. Looking at their faces, they could have been my neighbors, friends, or classmates. They were just like you and me. Nearly 90 percent of them were murdered in Nazi death camps.

I was a rising star in the NBA, but I walked out of the Holocaust Museum that day feeling insignificant. I had just borne witness to something so much bigger than myself. I knew what I had to do going forward. I was now on a mission. My plan was to use the Holocaust Museum as a vehicle to teach young people in positions of power why it's important to be inclusive and not exclusive. My hope was to show them that the Holocaust wasn't just a Jewish tragedy. It was a human tragedy.

Over my 18-year NBA career, whether I was playing for Milwaukee, Seattle, Boston, or Miami, I'd take someone to the Holocaust Museum whenever we were in D.C. They'd always thank me afterward. I could see in their eyes that their perspective had shifted. After my playing career ended, my education accelerated. I traveled to Poland and visited the site of the Warsaw Ghetto. I moved through the iron gates of Auschwitz and was consumed by the silence. Just stepping foot on that soil was chilling. Imagine walking the train tracks at Auschwitz where prisoners were offloaded. Or touring the barracks where prisoners were housed. Or entering the gas chambers where these innocent people were killed. The heaviness of it all was overwhelming. I can still feel it to this day. When I was appointed to the board of the Holocaust Museum by President Obama in 2016, it was an honor and responsibility I could never have imagined as that young kid watching *Schindler's List* in college.

All this time, despite immersing myself in Holocaust history, I was unaware of any connection between this horrible historical event and the game of basketball that had given me so much. I didn't realize that a family I've called my friends for more than 20 years actually *were* that connection. Sometimes it doesn't matter how well you know someone or how much time you spend with someone. There are always things that stay buried beneath the surface.

My relationship with the Grunfeld family started in 1999, when Ernie was named the general manager of our team, the Milwaukee Bucks. It was roughly a year after my first trip to the Holocaust Museum. Ernie came to the Bucks after having been a longtime NBA player and then the GM of the New York Knicks. He and I clicked instantly. He brought a New York City toughness that our team needed. I can still hear his heavy New York accent as he challenged us to demand excellence of ourselves and each other. I had no idea that English wasn't Ernie's first language and that most of his family had been killed in the same death camps that I'd studied over the years.

I vividly remember visiting Ernie at his new house once he'd settled in Milwaukee. He walked me past the many pictures of his wife, Nancy, his daughter, Rebecca, and his son, Dan. I had already gotten to know the family and could tell they were a tight-knit group. Ernie was committed to his wife and kids over everything else. Nancy was the rock. Becky was all smiles. Dan was a budding high school basketball player who was always shooting hoops at our practice facility. Whenever I'd give him advice about his game or a pair of shoes out of my locker, he was humble and grateful. They seemed like the quintessential American family. I didn't know about the history they all carried with them.

When Ernie showed me around his basement, he pulled out a few bins that contained the artifacts of his long and successful basketball career. There were jerseys, shoes, warmups, and other items. They were all nice and neat. I knew it was a life's pursuit contained in a few boxes, like mine would be one day. Ernie didn't say a word about his incredible origins or the tragedy he'd experienced before basketball. He didn't talk about his past, so I never knew the truth.

Now, I'm proud to stand with my friend Dan as he tells his astounding family story for the first time. Dan grew up to be a professional basketball player himself, but he is a writer at heart, and you'll see his gift on full display in this book. Ernie is the only NBA player whose parents survived the Holocaust, and in *By the Grace of the Game*, Dan is somehow able to make this complex journey from Auschwitz to the NBA come to life on every page. We're able to walk in the shoes of prisoners in concentration camps, of immigrants in America, and of generations of a family who were improbably saved by basketball. We're able to feel a son's unshakable commitment to his father and grandmother. And we're able to see how the tragedies of our past manifest in the generations that follow.

There's pain and heartache in this book, but at its core, it's about love, perseverance, and hope. This story is the embodiment of the American Dream. It shows why we should never stop fighting and never give up. It highlights why treating people right, taking care of each other, and embracing our differences will always matter most. It will help us remember that everyone we meet has a story we know nothing about. It's proof that we must continuously fight for the equality of every human being, no matter their gender, race, or religion.

The goals I used to set for myself in my playing days revolved around basketball. My main goal now is to spread love and human connection. I hope you feel this love as you read this one-of-a-kind story. It's a captivating and inspiring journey, as moving as it is miraculous, and I'm grateful that you're finally able to experience it. I know it will teach you a lot about hoops, about history, and ultimately, about the humanity that binds us all together.

Ray Allen is a 10-time NBA All-Star, a two-time NBA champion, and a Naismith Memorial Basketball Hall of Famer. Allen previously served on the board of the U.S. Holocaust Memorial Museum.

introduction

what matters most & why

ON MORE OCCASIONS THAN I'D LIKE TO ADMIT, I'VE become violently ill from my grandmother's Hungarian food. These unpleasant incidents have had nothing to do with contaminated ingredients or poor preparation. The truth of these mishaps is simple: my grandmother's cooking is so incredible that I can't stop eating it.

When I sense that her food is near, my eyes narrow and my heart soars, my every thought consumed by the impending flood of flavor. I lose all control. My mind goes blank, like an empty tray of her perfect pastries. I ignore that the pot will boil over and instead devote all my energy to feeling the heat. Despite the consequences — and believe me, they can be dire — I'm willing to exceed my body's capacity if it means I can keep tasting my grandmother's goodness. I've eaten myself sick from her food more than a dozen times, and I'll gladly do it a dozen more.

Rántott hús, meggyleves, piros krumpli, káposzta cosca, almas pite. I've been eating these dishes since I was a kid, a world away from where they originated. I didn't rise from the ashes like the rest of my family — I've lived a charmed life replete with any cuisine I could desire — but my grandma's traditional Hungarian food is what's always felt like home. They're the same meals her mother made for the family before they were murdered in the Holocaust. I know that by cooking them for me, my grandma feels connected to those she lost. The souls of her loved ones are gone, stripped from the bone in the most unimaginable of ways, but these sacred plates of food will live forever.

I call my grandma *Anyu*, which means "mother" in her native Hungarian. She calls me *tatele*, a Yiddish term of endearment, though she'll also refer to me as *kinchem, kichikinchem, apukum, drago, chilugem, shefele*, or *budesh kutcha*, which translated literally means "smelly dog."

When she speaks one of my nicknames, the words emanate from her gut. Most utterances live in the throat, but Anyu's *tateles* and *apukums* and *budesh kutchas* emerge from somewhere deep. They come out dripping with love. There's a gratitude to her affection, a sense that surviving the Holocaust taught her never to miss an opportunity to show her people how she feels about them.

For as long as I can remember, Anyu and I have talked on the phone every day, at one point or another. Wisdom has flowed freely during our calls, but only in one direction. When I've been nervous about where life might take me, Anyu has reminded me to stay focused on the work. When I've been disappointed in myself, she's encouraged me to view things from a different perspective. When I've been unable to handle the pressure, a common occurrence during my college and pro basketball careers, she's told me not to take things to my heart.

And when I've eaten myself sick at her apartment, she's flashed an easy smile, smoothed back her glowing white hair, and promptly offered me more food.

Conversations with older people can be limited in scope — the weather, gossip about the neighbors, dinner options, distant relatives, joint pain — but Anyu moves comfortably between politics, sports, her social life, career advice, and current events. The familiar tone of her voice produces a calming effect on me, though I know she's always been self-conscious about her accent. It's thick and rich, a melody I don't register after so many years of hearing it but one that's distinct and ever-present.

She's a Hungarian speaker from Romania, but her son, my dad, became a star in America. If the magnitude of an American Dream is measured by the intensity of the nightmare that came before and the heights of the triumph achieved after, then my dad has lived an American Dream story of unprecedented scale. He took our family from the grips of the Nazis to the top of the Olympic podium, from the cheap seats to center stage at Madison Square Garden, from yellow stars to silver spoons. He's the only player in NBA history whose parents survived the Holocaust.

Still, Anyu's accent serves as a small yet constant reminder of where they come from and the terrible things that happened there. I might not hear the accent, but I receive the reminder. The screams from Auschwitz echo across generations. The smoke still billows. It's impossible to blunt the realization that my family members were gassed to death and burned to nothing in ovens. They lived lives of passion and purpose but were turned into powder. That knowledge circles the spirit and is impossible to shoo away.

I was born into privilege, with advantages my ancestors couldn't have imagined, but I've never been able to separate my present from their past. The Holocaust and communism and life as refugees caring for a dying son in New York City are only the beginning. The true improbability of it all lies in the discovery of a game — the game of basketball — that unknowingly held the power to heal past wounds and tie a complicated history together, all the way from them to me. Our story is one of an ordinary family thrust into extraordinary circumstances. There's been darkness, but by the grace of God, there's also been basketball.

chapter 1

life & the city game

M Y BIRTH WAS PLANNED AROUND JUDAISM AND basketball. It's an appropriate testament to what I was inheriting. When I was born in 1984, my dad was an NBA player for the New York Knicks. My parents scheduled my C-section delivery to take place between two long road trips so he could be present for both my birth and my bris, the Jewish ritual of circumcision on the eighth day of life. I'm sure thousands of Jews in New York City during the 1980s planned their sons' bris ceremonies around Knicks games. My dad was almost certainly the only Jew actually playing in the Knicks game.

With my mom nine months pregnant, Dad embarked on a three-game trip to Texas to play the San Antonio Spurs, Dallas Mavericks, and Houston Rockets. On that trip, he watched his college running mate Bernard King score 50 points for the Knicks on back-to-back nights against San Antonio and Dallas. Dad can be seen on the bench in old videos of that second 50-point game, jumping up and down with his fists in the air and slapping five with his teammates. His shorts end mid-thigh. His hair ends at the shoulder. His mustache never ends. His improbable basketball career was drawing to a close by then.

After Texas, Dad played one home game against the Golden State Warriors at Madison Square Garden, scoring six points in 12 minutes. He was at the hospital when my birth was induced the following morning. He then hit the road to play in Utah, Denver, and Kansas City, returning from his second road trip eight days after I was born, just in time for my bris. He didn't rush back for my bris because he was particularly religious. He rushed back because it's a holy moment for a Jewish family. Besides, Anyu had knitted the yarmulkes — white with blue trim — and there was no way he'd disappoint her.

The ceremony was held at our home in northern New Jersey. The Carnegie Deli, New York's famous Jewish eatery, provided the corned beef and pastrami sandwiches on the house. They also threw in gefilte fish, pickles, chopped liver, the works. When a Jewish guy is a New York City basketball legend and an NBA player for the hometown Knicks, the Carnegie Deli will comp whatever the family noshes on for his son's bris. In New York City, that's a guarantee.

Family and friends gathered around, *kibitzing* quietly as they watched me get my penis snipped. Apu, my grandfather, held me as the mohel did his work. Anyu and Mom cried. The men cried, too, moved by the spiritual nature of it all. I'd entered into a covenant that Jewish parents had bestowed upon their sons for 3,000 years. Even the Holocaust couldn't break this tradition.

At the time, my dad wore No. 18 for the Knicks, a symbolic number in Judaism representing the word *chai*, which means "life" in Hebrew. New York City has the largest Jewish population in the world outside of Israel. My dad is the only Jewish player ever to wear No. 18 for the Knicks. One of my favorite pictures from my childhood involves that No. 18. It was taken at the end of my dad's playing career, after one of his Knicks practices. He's standing on the court wearing a white No. 18 practice jersey and blue Knicks sweatpants. He's barefoot, his thick ankles exposed, his size-16 feet planted onto the hardwood like tree stumps. He's 6'6", 235 pounds.

I'm standing on the court a few feet away from him, tiny and unassuming, a toddler dressed in jeans and a red sweater, a dark turtleneck underneath. I have miniature Nikes on my feet. My clothes are small enough to fit a large doll or a small human. I happened to be the latter.

The hoop hovers directly behind us. The basketball I'm holding is as big as I am. My arms and legs are tensed, as if I'm attempting to shoot the ball into the basket perched so high above me. I'm not yet two years old, but the basketball had been placed in my hands. From the very beginning, it felt important that I learn how to do something with it.

After his retirement from playing, when Dad was broadcasting games on the radio for the Knicks, he'd be invited to do shooting clinics at basketball camps around New York. Kids would ask where he was from. He'd always say New York City. Forest Hills, Queens, to be exact, right off of Continental Avenue, around the corner from the Austin Street Playground. It was impossible to tell that he'd fled a communist regime under duress and that English was his second language. He had no accent whatsoever. No one could have known that he still dreamt and counted in Hungarian.

During these clinics, Dad would teach proper mechanics on a jump shot — shoulders squared to the rim, elbow in, ball on the fingertips — before demonstrating himself. As he swished shot after shot, he told the crowd how easy shooting could be if you focused on the fundamentals. "I bet the smallest person here can shoot the ball like this as long as the technique is good," he'd say, peering into the throng of cross-legged campers. He'd point to the one kid who was tinier, skinnier, and sadder looking than the rest. "How about you?" he'd say to the runt. "Why don't you come up and demonstrate how to shoot the basketball the right way?"

I was scrawny and pale with a jagged bowl haircut and a cluster of misshapen freckles on each cheek. My protruding ears and rashy skin tied the unfortunate look together nicely. Just think about the boy in the movies who gets his head stuffed in the toilet by the older kids at school. Then think about the boy whose head *that* boy stuffs in the toilet. That was me.

Standing up and straightening my shorts, I'd weave through the pack and make my way up front. I wasn't part of the camp and had been planted in the crowd by my dad. I was roughly five years old. The real campers were 10 and up. I'd hear laughs and whispers as I approached the basket, being so frail and dorky compared to the bigger kids. Dad would flip me the ball and remind the crowd of the correct mechanics he'd displayed. There'd still be snickering as I positioned the ball in my hands. The instant my wrist snapped forward and the ball glided off my fingertips, arching and spiraling through space in precise harmony, its trajectory fixed on its destination, that snickering disappeared. That's when I learned how satisfying it could be to shut people up.

Dad had been working with me on my shot since I could walk. The form was pure, with the fingers evenly spaced and the guide hand expertly placed. The release was smooth and natural. My shot found the net over and over again. My performance helped my dad prove his point to the crowd: with the proper technique, anyone could shoot a basketball.

Even this little dipshit.

Man, I loved this game.

After broadcasting, my dad became an executive with the Knicks, and he'd take me to practice with him on the weekends, like he did when he was playing. We'd eat at the same diner afterward, always ordering cobb salads, no avocado, extra turkey. When it came to basketball, he schlepped me around everywhere. The game became our connective tissue, a love that tied us together. At home, he'd rebound for me in our driveway. I'd either listen when he gave me pointers, or I'd punt the ball into the woods and run inside. It could go either way, though I'd usually opt for the drama. There were stretches when I did more punting and running than a

Green Bay Packer. I'd always come back out once I'd calmed down, and he'd be waiting for me.

My dad never forced basketball on me and bragged to his friends about my grades, not my scoring average. He gave me the space and freedom to be whoever I wanted to be. I was the one who decided that I wanted to be like him. It was other people's eyeballs that intensified that pursuit.

In my room at night, I opened boxes of basketball cards, memorizing every stat off the back. I hid a flashlight under my pillow and read NBA history books beneath a blanket. I learned the life stories of the two players I most idolized: Michael Jordan and Larry Bird. Jordan had been cut from his high school varsity team as a sophomore, and Bird worked as a garbage collector in his hometown of French Lick, Indiana before enrolling at Indiana State for college. These guys became two of the greatest basketball players of all time. They were my proof that anyone could do anything. They were additional proof, at least, since I lived with the most extreme example and talked basketball with him constantly. When Dad got home from work at night, I'd always have the same request: "Ask me a trivia question!"

He'd take a deep breath, dropping his keys on the counter and loosening his tie. I was so annoying, but this was what he'd signed up for. He'd had me, he'd infected me with this fever, and now he'd have to deal with it, all day, every day. "Okay, but just one," he'd say, starting his way up the stairs. "Where did Oscar Robertson go to college?"

"Cincinnati," I'd quickly reply, following behind him. "Ask me another one."

"Fine," he'd say as I trailed him into the bedroom. "Who is the only player to lead the NBA in points and assists in the same year?"

"Nate Archibald," I'd say. "Another."

His brow would wrinkle. "I've already asked you every question I can think of," he'd say. "It's time to eat."

I had no choice but to comply. After dinner, he'd relocate to our den to put on a game. I'd position myself next to him to watch. Dad loved basketball as if it had pulled him out of a fire. It took most of my life to realize it had. When my older sister would come down the stairs in the morning, she'd see me sitting at the head of the kitchen table, feet up, reading the sports section of the *New York Daily News*. I'd cut the NBA box scores out of the paper and keep them in an old cigar box in my room.

My big sister wasn't as rabid about the game as I was, but we grew up in the same house, so it was just a way of life. In fourth grade, when her class assignment was to read an autobiography of an important historical figure and give a presentation for the class, she listened to her classmates share stories of Harriet Tubman, Abraham Lincoln, Amelia Earhart, and Ben Franklin. When it was her turn to present, my sister ran to the front of the room with a small basketball in her hand. She was wearing high-top sneakers, a Los Angeles Lakers jersey, and old athletic goggles. She released a picture-perfect skyhook and began rattling off facts about Kareem Abdul-Jabbar before the ball had even landed.

My childhood was full of love and laughter and basketball, though I struggled with my sensitivity. Over time, I developed a nervous tic in my eyes. I'd shift my eyes from side to side to release the tension, an unnatural motion for anyone, especially a little kid. My mom took me to get a brain scan, and all was fine. The tic was from stress. I was eight years old. A big part of my stress came from having a famous father who was great at what I needed to be great at. Being the child of a celebrity is fun, but there's a cost to it. Everyone you meet has expectations and motives. Everyone makes assumptions and judgements. These external pressures were only compounded by my naturally intense disposition.

As a baby, I'd scream until I'd vomit when I wanted to come out of my crib. As a toddler visiting the doctor's office to get a shot, I'd thrash so wildly and protest with such uncontrollable delirium that the doctors would have to put me in a straitjacket, a garment used to restrain mental patients and violent criminals. Based on my behavior at the doctor, that seemed like the very path I was headed down at that moment in my life.

One of my greatest sources of joy as a kid was my grandmother, Anyu. She lived in the Bay Area, all the way across the country, but she visited us often. My friends would hear Anyu's accent and ask where she was from. I was trained to say Romania, but that was the extent of it. I knew what the Holocaust was, but I hadn't yet been exposed to the details.

When she was in town, our lives revolved around food. The quantities and flavors defied comprehension. The ritual of gathering to eat as a family provided layers of nourishment. My dad sat at the head of our rectangular wooden table, serving as the epicenter for the swift rotations of *faschilt*, *piros krumpli*, *uborka*, and the rest. He and Anyu would exchange plates and communicate with each other in a language I didn't understand. I simply ate, and ate, and ate, unbothered by where that might lead me. One night I'd be lying on the couch after Anyu's dinner, the next I'd be lying on the bathroom floor. They were both fine by me.

Each day, Anyu would spend her evenings cooking in our kitchen, oil crackling in hot pans, her hands casting spells, an aroma of warmth floating through the house. When my dad got home from work, the hot Hungarian food would be waiting. Anyu would make sure to cook extra *rántott hús* for me so I could bring it to school for lunch and share it with absolutely no one.

Her white hair would be shining at the end of the driveway as the bus approached to drop me off after school. The New Jersey breeze was no match for her liberal application of Aqua Net hairspray. Her coif always stayed in place. One fall afternoon, as Anyu was rebounding for me in our driveway, the temperature dipped sharply. She begged me to go inside and put on a sweatshirt. For a Jewish grandmother, inadequately warm clothing is an open invitation to pneumonia, influenza, the plague, and quite possibly all three. Anyu would stop at nothing to get me to put on another layer. After protesting, I told her that if she could make a free throw, I'd run inside and get a sweatshirt. "Okay, give me two tries," Anyu said. "Throw me the ball."

I wasn't expecting that. She'd watched a lot of hoops in her day but had never shot a basket. She didn't even know how to hold the ball. She fingered the laces in an awkward motion before bringing the ball down below her waist to heave it underhand — or appropriately, granny style. The first shot barely hit the rim. She laughed and asked for the ball back.

She focused her eyes a little harder and bent a little lower. The second shot swished through the net. She threw her hands in the air and started clapping. She didn't care about the shot. It was the sweatshirt that had her heart soaring. As far as she was concerned, my life had just been saved. Deep down, I was happy her shot went in. It was fucking freezing out there.

The first time Anyu saw me play in an organized basketball game, I was in third grade, playing in a local rec league for fifth and sixth graders. My shorts looked like underwear and my jersey drooped over my bony frame. Sometimes, if the refs wouldn't call fouls when I drove to the hoop, I'd start crying. I might have scored 10 points on my best night before that game. When Anyu came to see me play, I had 24 points. I don't know how I scored so much, and I don't know why. I just know that I liked having Anyu there watching me.

chapter 2

Auschwitz & a spoon

WHEN ANYU RETURNED TO HER FAMILY HOME IN rural Transylvania in January 1945, her voice ricocheted off the walls. Everything in the house was gone, ransacked by looters. The laughter and conversation, the familiar hum of activity, it had all evaporated. A family of 12 had lived together in the house. Now, for the first time, Anyu was alone, without her parents and nine siblings.

She already knew that a brother had died in a camp in Ukraine, a sister had disappeared in Budapest, and two other siblings had survived. She still had no idea what had happened to the rest of her family. She would learn about it when her sister returned from Auschwitz, the only one to come back from the death camp. She'd receive the news that both of her parents and three of her siblings had been killed there.

The trains took them at the end of May 1944. They have no graves to visit and no death certificates to review. They were sent to Auschwitz and never heard from again. Anyu was 18 at the time. She was visiting her sister in Budapest when the Nazis invaded. Since Jews in Budapest were not sent en masse to the camps, she at least had the chance to fight for her life.

Before the Holocaust's new binary — die or survive — Anyu's childhood was symbolized by a fistful of sour cherries and overflowing pockets of porcini mushrooms. In the small village of Micula, Anyu's hometown in Romania on the border with Hungary, green fields were speckled with silver poplars in all directions. There was natural beauty but no running water, electricity, or cars. To be able to pickle a vegetable was to possess the greatest piece of technology the town had to offer. There were no newspapers or tele-visions and certainly no streaming videos or autonomous vehicles. Anyu insists life was happier that way.

Toilets were holes in the ground with makeshift wooden seats. The roads were paths carved through the mud by horse-drawn carts. The town's retail offerings reflected the core needs of humanity: three food markets and three bars. That was it. There was probably a brothel nearby, too. Just a hunch.

Anyu shared a room in the family home with her four sisters. Her five brothers had a room of their own. They were Orthodox, so the boys went to temple every Friday and Saturday. One of Anyu's brothers would sneak a novel into temple and slip it into his prayer book, preferring to read his stories rather than read the scripture. The girls prepared the food while the boys were at syna-gogue. Anyu and her sisters only attended services on Yom Kippur. The men sat downstairs at temple and the women sat upstairs. Anyu's father, Solomon, was an observant Orthodox Jew, but of the modern variety. He never grew the beard so common among Orthodox men, and he spent his free time in progressive pursuits such as playing chess and the violin. He was a successful landowner, employing a team of men who worked his property, growing plants and animals to be consumed by the family and sold to the commu-nity. On the land the men raised cows, turkeys, horses, chickens, sheep, ducks, and geese.

Each animal provided precise utility for the family. The cow gave milk. The turkey became a steady supply of meat. The horse lent its muscle for pulling wagons in the fields. The chicken was good for both meat and eggs, with its significance magnified by the contribution its carcass made to the soup, the *húsleves*, the staple of Shabbat dinner, a Friday night tradition for Jews around the world. Shabbat dinner took three days to prepare in Micula. Anyu's job was to pluck the feathers from the chicken one by one — a kosher preparation — after the kosher butcher had slaughtered the animal.

The sheep provided wool, an important income source, as well as milk, which my great-grandmother made into cheese. The duck offered a variety of gifts, including its meat for eating, its firm feathers for couch pillows, and its fat, known as *schmaltz*, for cooking. The goose was the headliner, its usefulness unquestioned and its prizes robust: there was meat, there was a heaping supply of *schmaltz*, there were plush feathers used to make bedroom pillows, and lastly, there was the liver — the fabled goose liver — one of the great culinary delicacies in Europe. Anyu's mother, Cecilia, would force-feed the goose to ensure the *foie gras* would be big and supple. The goose liver was so precious that it was never used to make the ordinary chopped liver served on Shabbat; duck, calf, or chicken livers were used instead. The goose liver was cooked separately with onions and served on toasted bread, melting away as it hit the heat of a hungry mouth.

Off the side of the house, in a large green orchard dotted with cherry trees, there grew carrot, parsley, tomato, pepper, eggplant, potato, zucchini, apple, plum, pear, lettuce, onion, scallion, cabbage, white mushroom, raspberry, gooseberry, and cherry. Every meal featured fruits and vegetables plucked fresh from the vine.

Leading up to the winter months, Anyu's mother would harvest enough *schmaltz* from both the ducks and the geese to last the entire season. She'd store the excess cooking fat in large containers. They'd rest in a cupboard next to premade jars of tomato sauce, an assortment of jams, and pounds of pickled cucumbers, pickled sauerkraut, pickled red cabbage, and other pickled vegetables. Fresh carrots and parsley were kept in buckets of sand, preserving the vegetables through the cold months.

In the spring, once the frost had gone and the cherry trees had bloomed, Anyu's parents would walk hand in hand after lunch, meandering their way through the endless maze of puffy white cherry blossoms. Anyu would lay out a blanket beneath the bright clouds of flowery folds, her nose buried in one of her father's books.

During the summer, meals were eaten as a family on the front patio under the silver Transylvania sky. My great-grandmother dressed the table with a white tablecloth, the kosher dishes arranged precisely, the polished silverware placed just right. The food was consumed family style. *Rántott hús, faschilt, cholent, piros krumpli, káposzta cosca, almas pite, meggyleves, húsleves.* It was traditional Hungarian food — breaded chicken breasts, beef and onion patties, meat stew, red potatoes, sautéed cabbage, apple squares, sour cherry soup, chicken soup — made from scratch. These are the dishes Anyu has always prepared for me. Every time I've told her she's the best cook that ever lived, which I've told her often, her response has been the same: "That's because you never ate my mother's cooking."

My great-grandfather sat at the head of the table and blessed the challah, baked fresh every Friday. Anyu was especially proud that her mother could braid the challah six times, not three like everyone else. When imported oranges were procured as a treat, my great-grandmother would fold the peel into the shape of a flower. When the tablecloth came off after dinner, a family dog, Tisa — big with white curly hair — would jump onto the table and sit for hours, watching over the house.

For adventure, Anyu would hike to a nearby field with some combination of her nine siblings — Shari, Margo, Ernie, Bubby, Bala, Andor, Eugene, Miki, and Heidi — to pick porcini mushrooms. For the rest of her life, she would order any dish at a restaurant if it contained porcini mushrooms. "Now, they're $22 a pound," I once heard her proclaim with a finger in the air as the server set down her meal, "but they used to be free!"

If Anyu couldn't be found at home, her family knew where to look. They'd walk out into the orchard and peer into the cherry trees, their leaves swaying under starry night skies. Anyu would be sitting on a branch, snapping cherries off the tree and popping them straight into her mouth. There was no war, no worries, and no notion of the darkness to come. Life was nothing more than a loving family, a tall tree, and an endless supply of sweet, juicy cherries.

Years later, it was my great-uncle Ernie, Anyu's oldest brother, who was the first to die in the Holocaust. He was poisoned to death in a labor camp in Ukraine. The guards had thrown meat to the prisoners, with starving men ripping at each other's clothes to secure a piece. The meat had been injected with poison. It was 1942. He was 25 years old.

My great-grandfather received the news on Shabbat, a Saturday. As an Orthodox Jew, he was strictly forbidden to read mail on Saturday. My great-grandfather had always abided by religious law, until then. He tore open the letter from the Red Cross and collapsed in tears when he learned that his son was dead. The stated cause of death was "exhaustion." A boy who'd survived the camp supplied the truth years later, after Anyu's dad was already gone.

My great-uncle Bala, Anyu's brother who read stories in temple, was summoned to a labor camp in Hungary, somewhere near Cluj. He was a prisoner with my future grandfather, a star athlete from Satu Mare, a neighboring city in Transylvania. Bala was never taken out of the country during World War II, or as Anyu would forever call it, "the War." He was liberated by the Russians in August of 1944 and would live and die in Israel.

My great-uncle Andor, or Andy as I knew him, was also taken to a labor camp in Hungary, likely near Budapest. He was transferred to the Budapest Ghetto near the end of the War. It was there that he was reunited with Anyu. It was there that his job was to collect dead Jews off the street, carry them into an abandoned building, and stack the bodies on top of each other in a crisscrossed pattern to ensure there was space for the others. After the War, he never talked about what he'd seen. Andy immigrated to New York City and worked in a leather factory. He died when I was a kid.

Two of Anyu's sisters, my great-aunts Shari and Margo, were in Budapest with Anyu when the Nazis invaded. It was March 1944. The letters from their parents stopped, and they'd heard that all Jews in Hungary, save Budapest, had been deported. Margo talked about going to Germany to try to find their parents. In her heart, she knew it wasn't possible.

Margo was caught by the Nazis and was one of the estimated 50,000 Jews on Adolf Eichmann's "death march" from Budapest to Vienna. The prisoners walked nearly 140 miles in a week to the outskirts of the Austrian frontier. We don't know if Margo survived the journey — nearly 10,000 are said to have died along the way — but we know she never made it home.

My great-aunt Bubby was the only family member to come back from Auschwitz. She was evaluated at the camp by Dr. Josef Mengele, known by history as the "Angel of Death." He took pleasure in deciding who'd live and who'd die. He'd hover as trainloads of prisoners arrived at Auschwitz, wearing his white doctor's coat and signature white gloves, looking for twins on whom he could experiment. When Mengele's shadowy eyes surveyed Bubby, he pointed to the right, indicating she was fit for labor. The prisoner before her, one of Anyu and Bubby's aunts, had been sent to the left — directly to the gas chambers. Bubby was transferred from Auschwitz to another camp and managed to stay alive until liberation.

Shari and Anyu both survived the War on the streets of Budapest. Shari would end up in Israel. Anyu ended up in the United States. The rest of Anyu's family — both parents and three siblings — were killed in Auschwitz. The trains from Transylvania started on May 19, 1944. My great-grandfather was deported on a train to Auschwitz. His name was Solomon Samuel, but I would have called him *Nagypapa*, pronounced "nudge-papa."

Before his murder, Nagypapa dressed in a three-piece suit and tracked the schedules of his 10 kids from the pocket watch dangling on his hip. He attended temple every day and spoke Hungarian, German, and Yiddish. He was educated at the Pressburg Yeshiva in Bratislava, one of the most prestigious schools in Europe. He played the violin and spent hours each day reading from his collection of classic books. On Saturday evenings, under the light of a petroleum lamp, he'd sit at a handmade wooden table and play chess with a friend until the early morning. His education and integrity made him a leader in his village's Jewish community. When the region's most renowned rabbi visited town for a religious ceremony, Nagypapa was given the honor of hosting the distinguished guest in his home. Anyu still remembers the great Rabbi Joel Teitelbaum blessing her and her siblings in the family kitchen before the ceremony commenced.

Almost a century later, Netflix would release a hit series called *Unorthodox* profiling the Satmar Jews, the ultra-Orthodox sect that Rabbi Teitelbaum started when he fled Romania for Brooklyn before the War. Anyu wouldn't have been able to comprehend the notion that this man's approach to Judaism could inspire a global television phenomenon. At the time of her first interaction with Rabbi Teitelbaum, she'd never before seen a television.

My great-grandfather was also revered in town for his wisdom. When a Jewish neighbor sold a parcel of land to buy his wife the fur coat she demanded, the decision was panned as senseless and short-sighted. *Why would he mortgage their future to satisfy this compulsion? What is he thinking selling land to get a coat?* "Maybe it is senseless, maybe it isn't," Anyu recalls her father saying, opposing the common sentiment in the community. "Time will tell."

Years later, the Nazis came, and all land was taken. At least the fur coat had brought enjoyment and happiness when those things were still possible. Somehow, Nagypapa knew not to rush to judgment. It speaks to perspective and humility — to acknowledging that no one has it all figured out.

My great-grandfather, Solomon, was my hero's hero. When the Nazis loaded him onto the train, Anyu's father was 56 years old. Historical accounts of the Holocaust make it possible to reconstruct my family's deportation with a high probability of accuracy. On the way to Auschwitz, with people piled on top of one another inside the slatted wooden cattle car, there was no food, no place to go to the bathroom, and nowhere to lay down. Human waste piled up. The smell was overpowering. The ride lasted days. Many prisoners died on the train from hunger, suffocation, or illness. I think Nagypapa survived the journey, driven by his instinct to protect his family. His wife, daughter, and two sons were on the train with him. Accounts of Auschwitz suggest that, after Nagypapa arrived at the death camp in the south of Poland, he was offloaded onto a ramp and corralled by shouting SS officers into a line for men. That's when he was separated from his wife and daughter — my great-grandmother and great-aunt.

My great-uncles, Anyu's little brothers, stayed with their dad. He held them close as they averted their eyes from the SS officers and moved forward in line. They eventually reached a man wearing a white coat. At his age, Nagypapa was not fit to do hard labor. My great-uncles, both small and undeveloped, were just young teenagers. The German physician took a quick look and pointed to the left. The Nazis had for years disguised their murderous activities as a resettlement campaign, so information about what was happening to Jews at these camps was still scarce across Europe. My great-grandfather was likely unaware of what was coming.

Nagypapa and my great-uncles were brought to a building that said "bath" in a variety of different languages. They were stripped and led inside along with hundreds of other naked Jews. Doors were shut behind them. There were shower heads on the walls, but once the doors were locked, gas started to seep from the vents. By the time Nagypapa realized what was happening, it was much too late. He was probably holding his boys until the end.

When Auschwitz was liberated and the walls of the gas chambers examined, they were filled with fingernail scratch marks. After the male prisoners had been killed — Nagypapa and my great-uncles included — rings were removed, and gold was pulled from teeth. The bodies were then sent to the crematoria, where my great-grandmother and great-aunt's corpses had also been taken. As arriving prisoners at Auschwitz pleaded not to be separated from their loved ones, the Nazi guards were trained to say, "You'll be together again soon." It was an unfathomable truth.

All the bodies were placed into an oven and burned into ash. That ash was propelled out of a tall gray chimney. It floated to a universe far better than our own.

Unaware of all that had happened, Anyu returned to her empty house after surviving the War in Budapest. Her head throbbed. The white tablecloths, the silver, the kosher dishes, the bedroom pillows stuffed to the brim with goose feathers — it was all gone. There were no animals on the farm. The crops were decimated.

Anyu's steps were slow as she walked around the house. Examining empty drawer after empty drawer, she eventually noticed something shimmer. Somehow overlooked by the looters, it was wedged in the back of one of the drawers. It was one of my great-grandmother's spoons. Used in the kosher household for ladling milk, the spoon was small, metallic, and nondescript. The handle was worn, the bowl weathered and scratched. The spoon had either gone unnoticed by the looters or, more likely, possessed so little value that it was left behind without a thought. Anyu grabbed it from the drawer and held it to her heart. Aside from what remained inside her, this spoon was all that was left. She would have it in her possession for 75 years before giving it to me. I keep it in my bedside drawer, a few feet from where I sleep.

chapter 3

The Garden & beasts

THE NEW YORK KNICKS TEAMS OF THE EARLY 1990S, the ones I grew up around, were the beating heart of New York City. The players weren't fit for the palm trees in Los Angeles or the sand beaches of Miami. They embodied the hard hats and honking horns of the five boroughs. They were a graffiti and subway steam type of group. Barbed-wire fences. Sewer rats as big as house cats.

My dad was the general manager of the Knicks, having gone from player to broadcaster to assistant coach to running the team in the span of a few years. He was raised in the shadows of the Holocaust, eating black market meat and going to the bathroom in an outhouse. He'd been a poor immigrant learning English in New York City. Then the city became his city. It was an extraordinary trajectory for a Hungarian-speaking Jew from Communist Romania.

In those days, being GM of the Knicks made you a king in New York. I benefited from this stature, even though I hadn't earned any of it. I was a typical prince born into good fortune. To relate, I tried to conceal my lifestyle from peers at school. I always felt most comfortable around other Knicks kids, since they understood. When the New York Yankees played in the World Series, our family would have seats on the dugout. We'd attend *Saturday Night Live* premieres, where I'd have a 30-second conversation with Jim Carrey at an afterparty and immediately declare my childhood a success. I was once the only person skating on the rink at Rockefeller Center during a Knicks holiday party. I glided across the ground with a grin as scarf-wrapped tourists peered down at me, the world's most iconic Christmas tree lighting the night sky above, my blades shaving the New York City ice to dust.

Around that time, I'd dropped out of Hebrew school to accommodate my basketball schedule. I was on multiple traveling teams and would usually leave Temple Beth Rishon early so I could play in some game. When sitting in my basketball uniform at Hebrew school as I stared at the clock became untenable, my parents hired a private tutor to come to our house once a week to prepare me for my Bar Mitzvah. I don't know where my parents found Mrs. Brandeis, my persistent Torah practitioner, but I endured her weekly visits. At 4'10" with a scratchy voice and a tenacious love for the Talmud, Mrs. Brandeis stayed patient as I struggled to read Hebrew. I couldn't understand whose idea it was to have Hebrew written right to left. It all felt backward, like a soak with no *schvitz*, and I told her so. She somehow kept me focused long enough to teach me my Torah portion.

On Knicks game days, I was the young smartass running around Madison Square Garden, greeting security guards and asking how their families were, as if that were a normal thing for a kid to do in the world's most famous arena. I was social and gregarious, the type who seemed destined to one day shake hands and kiss babies, and I schmoozed at The Garden like it was a goddamn professional networking event. "Marge make the meatloaf this week?" I'd ask Tony outside section 107. "How's Bobby's fastball?" I'd ask Chuck while passing 110.

I'd sit in a team lounge before the game and chat with Red Holzman, Dad's mentor and the greatest coach in Knicks history. A jersey with his name on it was already retired at The Garden to commemorate his 613 wins as coach of the Knicks. Whenever I'd say good-bye to Red, he'd always tell me the same thing: "Remember, Danny, 10 percent." Red knew I loved the game and thought I had a chance to be good. He said he was going to be my agent, and all it would cost me was 10 percent.

Anyu came to a few games a year during her visits from California. She chased me around The Garden and knew the stadium cold. The security guards greeted her with deferential smiles, not just because she was the boss' mother. No matter how brief, her every interaction conveyed a profound kindness and respect. People felt her sublime energy and treated her accordingly.

Madison Square Garden, the home of the Knicks, had an unmistakable smell, something like pretzels, beer, and time. Its atmosphere held the weight of what its walls had seen. John Lennon, Wayne Gretzky, Willis Reed, Rocky Marciano, Michael Jordan, Andre the Giant, Muhammad Ali, Biggie Smalls, Barbara Streisand, Bernard King. Anyone who was anyone in sports and entertainment had made a name for themselves at Madison Square Garden.

New York is a basketball city, so nothing could tap into the heart of the people like the Knicks. Whether in a Knicks jersey or a pinstripe suit, a Knicks fan at The Garden was never more than a minute away from unleashing a screaming barrage of expletives on the other team. I once walked into The Garden before a Knicks playoff game to find the arena packed with fans already chanting New York's famous refrain of "Deee-fense, Deee-fense." The game was an hour away from starting. The players were still in the locker room. The fans were simply out of their minds.

My dad watched these games from a box at the top of the arena. He made sure I sat next to him. As a kid, not long after coming to America, he'd watched Knicks games with his dad from the top of the old Garden. They sat in the rafters where they belonged, not in a skybox reserved for team executives. They were still learning the language then.

Dad's Knicks, meanwhile, were perennial title contenders. They'd make the NBA Finals in 1994. Their identity was toughness. They were a group of fighters and survivors. They were used to overcoming challenges and overpowering odds. None of his players knew the details of Dad's background, but it didn't matter. He was one of them, and they were just like him.

Xavier McDaniel, known as X-man, shaved both his head and his eyebrows to look more intimidating, an act the locals might have referred to as "commitment."

John Starks, the Knicks' shooting guard, went to four colleges in Oklahoma and was bagging groceries at a Piggly Wiggly before making an NBA roster. He'd pound his chest after a made three and dive headfirst into the stands for a loose ball. He was raw and emotional, a guy New York City could believe in. He'd become an All-Star with the Knicks.

From Springfield Gardens, Queens, Anthony Mason started his career in Turkey, Venezuela, and the minor leagues. He boldly shaved images into his head throughout the season. Mase would run out of the tunnel with a Knicks logo on the side of his head or the skyline of New York City wrapping around his skull. Despite his humble beginnings, he'd also become an NBA All-Star.

Charles Oakley, from Cleveland, played his college ball at Virginia Union University. When he needed stitches during a Knicks game, he'd get them without Novocain. He used to cut a slit into the top of his practice jersey because his chest was so big. People called him Oak, and it made sense.

When Oak joined the Knicks, Dad was broadcasting for the team. On a chartered plane ride, a veteran teammate threw a peanut at the back of Oak's head. Oak told him not to do it again. Another peanut bounced off. Oak told him that if it happened one more time, there'd be a problem. A minute later, another peanut hit. Oak calmly stood up, walked a few rows back, and buried his fist into his teammate's mouth. Blood splattered onto the seat. "Bet you won't do it again," Oak murmured as his teammate tried to put his face back together. Dad was sitting several rows behind and saw the whole thing. Without saying another word, Oak returned to his seat and resumed the flight. I'm not sure if he asked the flight attendant to bring him a bag of peanuts when he sat down, but I'm not ruling it out. He was a good match for New York City.

Patrick Ewing, the Knicks' franchise player, played so hard and sweat so much that ball boys were given special instructions to mop the puddles that formed anywhere Patrick stood on the court. Patrick's rookie year with the Knicks was my dad's last as a player. Patrick carried Dad's bags on the road even though he was the first pick in the draft on a clear path to NBA superstardom. Dad calls him a warrior, one of the best and hardest working players he's ever been around. He was an immigrant, too, from Jamaica. He became one of New York City's very own.

Growing up, I eventually ran out of space for Knicks paraphernalia on the walls of my room. I'd gotten a bowling pin at a birthday party that I used as a hammer to hang posters, jerseys, magazine covers, and anything else that had a Knicks logo on it. With no spots left on the wall, I'd stand on a little blue swivel chair, grab my bowling pin and thumbtacks, and pound life-sized cutouts of the players' faces into my ceiling. When I lay in bed at night, the rough and rugged Knicks stared down at me.

At Knicks practice with my dad on the weekends, the players would give me fist pounds and ask how my jumper was coming along. I'd sit on the side and study them. I'd watch their moves, their mannerisms, how they worked. I'd try those things in my driveway. I wanted to play in the NBA like them. More than anything, I wanted to be tough like them, or at least perceived as tough. It was a difficult proposition for a scrawny Jewish kid from the right side of the tracks. The most challenging circumstance I'd faced until that point was when my sister finished the lox and bagels before I woke up one Sunday.

Every summer, I attended Knicks basketball camp at Manhattan College in the Bronx. As I got older, my game progressed, and I became one of the best players in my age group. Each session of camp ended with an awards ceremony that coincided with family pickup. I played particularly well one week, leading my team to the championship and being named MVP of my age group. When they called my name to accept my awards, parents looked around, incredulous, then started booing me. "He's the GM's kid!" one yelled. "We didn't spend our money for this crap!" another said.

Whenever adults openly berate a child, it's a hard thing to justify, though I understand the frustration. It didn't matter where my family had come from. I myself was privileged and had advantages other kids didn't. I get why parents would think my awards were a gift. I decided it was my responsibility to leave no doubt about what I did and did not deserve.

My education on the nature of humanity was accelerated by the anti-Semitism I experienced, as all Jews do, simply by being Jewish. By this time, I knew what had happened to Anyu and her family during the Holocaust. Still, I saw firsthand that certain people would hate me because I was Jewish. I'd been called "Jew boy" by kids at school. I'd heard a classmate say "Jew me down" to describe someone trying to buy an item from him at a low price. Jokes about Jews — cheap, big noses, dishonest — were commonly told.

I once opened a blue baseball shed in my hometown in New Jersey and saw a giant white swastika painted on the inside of the door. The paint was fresh. My heart nearly stopped. I'd seen that twisted symbol before and knew what it meant. I had a constant awareness that anti-Semitism lingered even when it wasn't apparent to the naked eye. It was one of the world's strongest parasites. How could that much hatred just disappear? Where would it go?

More and more, I wanted to be a Jew who dominated on the basketball court. As a player, my dad was big, strong, and unstoppable. There was not much anyone could say about that. To meet this end, I started working on my game obsessively, sometimes until my hands would bleed. If being Jewish and the son of an NBA player made me feel different, then being disciplined and determined made me feel defiant. I was used to kids at school teasing me about being Jewish or taunting me if the Knicks lost. I couldn't change that, but I could make them wish they'd never played ball against me.

I'd invite kids over from the neighborhood so I could beat their asses in basketball. If I played a friend one-on-one, I'd insist they'd need to score 11 to win and I'd need to score 33. They'd complain, aware of the blatant disrespect I was showing, but I'd refuse to play unless they'd agree. They'd agree, and I'd win. And I'd tell them next time I'd play to 50. I became resolute and brash because I felt advantaged and judged. Most displays of bluster are driven by insecurity and anger. Mine were no different.

My freshman year in high school coincided with the 1998-99 NBA season, my dad's 17th with the Knicks. It was delayed due to a lockout. I was 5'10", 145 pounds, playing on the freshman basketball team at the local high school. Not the junior varsity or varsity team. The freaking freshman team. Despite my lowly status, I consistently made the outrageous claim that I was going to play college basketball at Stanford University, right near Anyu in California. The Cardinal had been to the Final Four the year before, and Stanford was one of the best schools in the world. I'd been saying for years that I would play at Stanford. Kids would laugh in my face, and I don't blame them.

Before the NBA season started, with expectations for the Knicks at an all-time high, Dad made several controversial trades to try to improve the team. He moved franchise fixtures Charles Oakley and John Starks out of New York in exchange for high-risk, high-reward younger players. He sent Oakley to the Toronto Raptors for Marcus Camby, the former second pick in the draft whose career had stalled, and Starks to the Golden State Warriors for Latrell Sprewell, the All-Star who'd been suspended from the NBA for choking his coach during practice. In New York, it's not about winning; it's about winning big. Dad rolled the dice.

As the season got underway, the Knicks hovered around .500, an unacceptable record for a club of their stature. The players looked disjointed, and the spirit of the group seemed sour. The compressed timeline of the season created more pressure than usual. The New York media latched onto that pressure, sucking out every ounce of intrigue and controversy it could find.

Pundits started to point fingers. I'd wake up in the morning to see my dad's face on the cover of the newspaper, accompanied by a feature article detailing why he should be fired from his job. It would be written by someone with no true understanding of the situation and with no hands-on experience in the field being discussed. The conventional wisdom in media is "if it bleeds, it leads," and when it came to my dad, they were out for blood.

Anyone with a prominent family member has had to deal with this type of vitriol at one point or another. I felt bad for everyone involved: my dad, my family, and the people who'd cheapened themselves by making a living bringing others down. I'd seen the dark side of the New York City media before — when I was younger, reporters used to call my house and try to trick me into telling them what trades my dad was working on — but this storm was different. The onslaught of negativity from the media was relentless. Dad stayed above it and never said a bad word to the press.

On April 19, 1999, the Knicks fell to the Philadelphia 76ers, their fourth loss in a row. Sprewell and Camby both came off the bench, playing limited roles. The following night, unbeknownst to me, Dad's boss and best friend invited him to dinner at an Italian restaurant in White Plains, New York. There were eight games left in the regular season. The Knicks were an even 21-21. Both my dad and the coach were in the media's crosshairs, but Dad's boss constantly assured Dad he had his back.

After a meal spent discussing how to fix the team, just as dessert had been served, my dad was fired. His 17 consecutive seasons with the Knicks, a family journey that had started in Auschwitz, ended right there, with Dad as a scapegoat. The New York media would eventually call this dinner "The Last Supper." When Dad got home that night, I was sleeping under the stars on my ceiling. He and my mom decided they'd tell me the news the following day. This one had already been traumatic enough.

Earlier that morning, at Columbine High School in Littleton, Colorado, two seniors wearing black trench coats and carrying semi-automatic rifles had opened fire on their classmates in the first mass school shooting of my generation. The shooters murdered 12 students and one teacher, eventually taking their own lives in the school library. The killers had planned their massacre for April 20. They wanted to carry out their attack on Adolf Hitler's birthday.

The day after Columbine, my guidance counselor popped his head into my last class, biology, and asked me to stop by his office when school ended. I knew something was up. When the bell rang, I blew past my locker and weaved through the crowd. Before I could get to my guidance counselor's office, the sea of students parted, and there was my mom. Her bright blonde hair stood out immediately. As soon as she saw me, tears ran down her cheeks. I looked at her and nodded my head. "Let me get my stuff," I said.

The first thing she told me in the car was that it was okay to cry. And I did. I cried. She also told me that my guidance counselor said I didn't have to come to school the next day. It was okay if I needed time to process this on my own.

It was a nice offer, but fuck that.

I'd lost something I loved, but people were going to see my face the next morning. The greatest lesson Anyu had ever taught me was that it's not about what happens to you in life; it's about how you respond to what happens to you. I talked to her for a while the night I found out my dad was fired. She told me it would be okay. I believed her.

The Knicks ended up winning six of their last eight regular-season games that year, barely making the playoffs as the No. 8 seed in the East. Due to injuries to other players, Sprewell and Camby both saw their roles increase, and the team started to click. The vision started to come together. Just like that, The Garden sprung back to life. The team Dad had been fired for assembling made it to the NBA Finals that year. Some fans at The Garden wore masks of his face to games as a tribute. Someone paid for a billboard in New York City that read "Bring Back Ernie." None of it mattered. He was done in New York. He'd already been sacrificed.

The Knicks lost in the Finals in five games to the San Antonio Spurs. Dad watched the Finals in our basement, in the dark. For him, the Knicks had been a dream conjured in the rafters of the old Garden by a boy leaning on basketball to practice his English and heal from tragedy. The dream was over. For me, the Knicks had been my reality since the day I was born. That was over, too, vanished in a puff of smoke. What was left was fire, burning hotter now, fueled by obligation, stoked by anger. I was 15 years old, skinny, Jewish, and mad. I spent more time than ever in the driveway, working on my game.

chapter 4

soup & Nazis

ANYU SAT ON THE TRAIN. IT WAS 1943. SHE WAS 17. IN her family's orchard in Micula, the gold-beaked bramblings fluttered through her cherry trees. Across Europe, the German Luftwaffe hummed over the heads of civilians, their wings holding steady, their bombs eager to wipe life away.

The Nazis had long since tightened their chokehold on Europe by invading the Soviet Union in June of 1941. The method to murder Jews up to that point had been mass shootings by killing squads. The Nazis quickly discovered that this type of murder was costly and slow. Thousands of Jews at a time were forced to dig their own graves before being lined up and gunned down. To smooth out their death machine, the Nazis developed mobile gas vans to complement mass exterminations by machine gun. Exhaust pipes on paneled trucks were reconfigured so poisonous carbon monoxide gas was pumped into sealed spaces, killing everything locked within.

Emboldened by this clean new murder mechanism, the Nazis authorized what is known as the Final Solution: the systematic elimination of Jews. Chelmno, the first killing center in Nazi-occupied Poland, had three functioning gas vans. The next three killing centers in Poland, at Belzec, Sobibor, and Treblinka, were all equipped with stationary gas chambers. Auschwitz, where my family was killed, had four large gas chambers. Each of them could facilitate the murder of 2,000 people at a time.

In September of 1941, a thousand prisoners were jammed into the basement of Block 11 at Auschwitz, known as the "death block," as if this area deserved distinction from the rest of the camp. Adolf Eichmann and other top Nazi officials were searching for a faster way to kill than carbon monoxide. As a test, Zyklon B was released inside the chamber of Block 11. To the satisfaction of the Nazi leaders, all the prisoners died within minutes.

Zyklon B was a hydrogen cyanide-based fumigant used to disinfect ships and factories and to kill rats and insects. The Zyklon B pellets were a breezy amethyst blue color. When exposed to air, they turned shockingly lethal. They were stored and transported in hermetically sealed canisters as a precaution. In Auschwitz, the Zyklon B was simply dropped into the gas chambers. The poison that blossomed from these mystifying azure pellets was pure evil. After the War, the British hanged Bruno Tesch, Zyklon B's inventor and supplier. His name is a footnote in history. A million people choked on what he made.

Anyu was unaware these things were happening. She didn't fully comprehend what she'd soon be running from. There was no electricity in Micula, so radio access had been infrequent. They had radios in nearby Satu Mare, but the information was limited. Nazi propaganda confused everyone. No one knew what to believe. As the train wheels rattled, the big city came into view. The train to Budapest was always crowded, but Anyu didn't arouse suspicion. Jews were said to have dark hair and bent noses. Anyu was blonde and pretty.

Before Anyu set off for Budapest, Hungarian soldiers had been pulling Jewish girls off trains in Transylvania and raping them. Since everyone knew Anyu in Micula, her father forbade her from taking the train to the nearby high school like her sisters had. She settled for her father's books and lessons from an educated neighbor. Her father had attended one of the best yeshivas in Europe, but Anyu's only option for education was to read everything in sight. It never felt like enough.

Anyu was on her way to Budapest to visit her older sister, Shari, and to find a job. Her brothers were already in labor camps and the oldest, Ernie, was dead. Still, her early months in Budapest were idyllic. Hungary, a conservative aristocratic government sympathetic to the Nazis, had so far refrained from rounding up its Jewish citizens, and anti-Jewish laws couldn't be imposed on someone who no one knew was Jewish. Anyu strolled Budapest's tree-lined streets and visited the banks of the Danube. She blended easily into cafes and restaurants. She walked the park with her sister, admiring the flowers. She didn't hear much about the Nazis. War was raging, but people in Budapest went about their daily lives. Anyu got a job trimming leather in a pocketbook factory. The work was tedious and precise, a perfect fit.

Things changed on March 19, 1944. After learning of Hungary's secret armistice conversations with the Allies, the Nazis invaded. Anyu was staying with two of her sisters, Shari and Margo, by then. Almost instantly, German tanks rumbled across the Hungarian border, and planes hummed overhead. Anyu looked out the window on the day of the invasion and saw Nazis on the street with machine guns. They were shouting at civilians and interrogating passers-by. She heard rumors of Jews being hanged. She shut the window and kept it closed. The air grew thick. The sisters spoke in low, anxious tones. Northern Transylvania had been transferred from Romania to Hungary in the Second Vienna Award in 1940, so their hometown of Micula was now also under German control.

A letter from their father arrived in the first post after the invasion. Its contents were simple, a curt message delivered through clean cursive: *come home immediately*. Anyu's heart thumped. She and her sisters packed their suitcases and organized their belongings. They stayed inside and hardly slept. The next day, as they made their final preparations for the trip home, another letter arrived. It contained an equally simple message from their father: *stay there if you can.* It wasn't until after the War that Anyu understood that this second letter had saved her from Auschwitz.

Her father had panicked at first but quickly realized that his daughters had a better chance of surviving in a big city. Few people knew who they were in Budapest, and there were at least nooks and crannies to hide in. That letter was Anyu's last contact with her beloved father, Solomon.

As soon as the Nazis occupied, they went door-to-door in Budapest to locate the enemy. Jews were still not being deported, merely corralled and catalogued in preparation for future action. Anyu and her sisters had a chance of convincing the Nazis they were gentiles. Jewish boys were all circumcised, a rarity in Europe in those days and thus a clear indicator of Jewish identity. Anyu and her sisters bore no mark of the faith, but the Nazis had done their homework. They went through housing records. They talked to gentile neighbors and promised them the discarded belongings of Jews in exchange for information. They were trained to withhold the benefit of the doubt and consider everyone a Jew unless proven otherwise. Being blonde and pretty wasn't enough.

Anyu's breath halted when she heard a sharp bang on the door. She creaked it open to reveal three Nazis standing over her. The faces of the young men were immaculately shaven, their boots laced high and tight. When they spoke, their voices were strong and self-assured. Their confidence was warranted: these men had the backing of the most powerful death apparatus the world had ever seen. They demanded identification from all the sisters and scanned the documents with focused eyes. One let out a smirk. They already knew the Samuel girls were Jewish. Anyu was kicked out of the apartment and given a bright yellow Star of David badge. "Wear it at all times," one of the Nazis muttered in Hungarian.

With nowhere to live, Anyu and her sisters got word of a house in Budapest with a yellow star above the door. It was owned by a Jew who'd converted it into small apartments. It was a "Star of David" house, a lodging where displaced Jews could find shelter. It would provide a roof over their heads, but with so many Jews centralized in one location, it would make them easy targets when things got worse.

The three sisters had a room the size of a large closet. They shared the one twin bed inside. They had a blanket and a few pillows. It was the best they could do. When they started noticing the Nazis knocking on doors and hauling people off, they waited to see when the apprehended would return. They soon learned the answer, in every instance: never.

They split their time between the Jewish house and a bombed-out building nearby. The accommodations in the bombed-out building were not nearly as good as in the Jewish house — they slept on the floor in the building with only their winter coats to cover them — but neither place was safe. Diversifying felt like the right strategy. They were forced to rely on strangers for food. A Hungarian army commander was kind and provided an occasional bite to eat. Nonetheless, they were always hungry. The feeling was a cruel departure from the bountiful family meals prepared by their mother. Anyu tried and failed to get used to it.

When Anyu huddled in corners with other Jews in Budapest, she kept hearing about Raoul Wallenberg. He was a young and wealthy Swedish diplomat who'd come to Budapest to try to save the Jews. Instead of destroying life, someone was finally trying to preserve it. Wallenberg wasn't even Jewish; he was simply a man of honor. Anyu was reminded of her father. She wondered where he was.

Through the Swedish embassy, Wallenberg was issuing protective passports to Jews in Budapest. They were called Schutz-Passes.

They identified the possessors as Swedish subjects awaiting repatriation. The Schutz-Pass wasn't a legal document, but it looked legitimate and had the backing of a neutral foreign government. It was significant enough to prevent eventual deportation by the Germans and Hungarians upon capture.

As soon as Anyu learned of the Schutz-Pass, she walked the streets of Budapest to find the Swedish Embassy. Nazis had been pulling people out of line at the embassy and arresting them, she knew, but she took the risk. She asked careful question after careful question until she eventually reached her destination. Her eyes bulged when she arrived. The queue was massive, stretching all the way down the street.

With a deep breath, she took her place in line. Her eyes darted. She waited for hours, inching forward a few feet at a time, until she got inside the embassy. Swedish officials asked her for her papers. She told them her identification was back at the Jewish house. To Anyu's surprise, the Swedes handed her a note allowing her to bypass the line once she returned to the embassy with her documents.

Finally, an opportunity.

The very next day, Anyu was back at the embassy to get her Schutz-Pass. She asked for a few extras, too, because there would never be a better time to press her luck. The Swedish officials obliged, handing Anyu a few extra passes. Better still, they never reclaimed the note allowing Anyu to skip the line. She didn't say a word. Her sisters were now taken care of, and she had a ticket to the embassy door.

Over the following week, Anyu made the treacherous walk to and from the embassy five times, procuring 17 passes to distribute. She gave them all away, mostly to people she'd met while hiding but also to a few strangers who just needed help. These passes were valuable on the streets, but she never considered selling them. It wasn't how her father had raised her.

Even with a Schutz-Pass in her possession, Anyu was required to wear her yellow star on her clothes everywhere she went. Like most Jews, she was only allowed to be on the streets from 11:00 AM to 2:00 PM. A few Jews had working permits and could go out during the day for longer stretches, but Anyu wasn't one of them.

Since she needed money, she left her Star of David badge behind and snuck into the city in search of work. The streets were chaos, but everything at the time was chaos. There seemed to be a Nazi on every corner, so Anyu kept her head down and her eyes to herself. She was still hiding, only this time in plain sight.

She found work in a champagne factory, a modest operation of 10 or so people. Her job was to load syrup into the champagne bottles. At lunchtime, she was given a glass of champagne as a treat. She made sure to put a lot of syrup in it. She liked it sweet.

After a few restless months, Wallenberg's Schutz-Pass became meaningless when a pro-Nazi Hungarian government led by Ferenc Szálasi was installed to replace the moderate party of Miklós Horthy. With her insurance now gone, Anyu stayed at the Jewish house less and less, fearing the Nazis' presence. Sometimes she hid with her sisters; sometimes she did not. It was easy to get separated for weeks at a time.

As the days wore on, food became even harder to come by. The champagne factory had been shut down since the owner was Jewish, so Anyu no longer had a job. The owner and his wife started hiding in the bombed-out building. They sometimes slept on the floor near Anyu.

With war consuming Europe, bomb blasts from advancing Allied forces were common in the evenings. One night as Anyu hid, she heard bursts of sound that were lighter and less threatening, as if born from the sky instead of driven into the ground. She noticed other hiding Jews making their way onto the street. She followed. When she emerged into the cool night air, brilliant flashes reflected off her eyes. She looked around at her fellow Jews as they gazed up, dirty, hungry, and tired. For the first time in a long time, she saw smiles. Fireworks rained down from the sky like golden chandeliers, illuminating a dark and destroyed city. Her mouth ajar, Anyu admired the display for several minutes until an unmistakable boom shook the ground. Anyu's features tightened. The Jews ran back to their hiding places to seek cover from the bombs. Anyu learned later that it was a common Ally tactic to light up the sky with flares to get better visuals on targets before initiating a bombing raid. For a few minutes, at least, she again saw beauty.

Not long after, Anyu's friend's boyfriend, a Jew, stole a Nazi uniform and acquired fake papers indicating he was a young German soldier. With these items, he was able to legally rent an apartment outside the city. Anyu had been separated from her sisters for weeks and wasn't safe anywhere. She moved in with her friend and the boyfriend, even though she thought the boyfriend was trouble. Days later, the boyfriend went to a non-Jewish friend's house to have a drink. Lips loosened by the spirits, he confessed to the friend and his wife that he was a Jew. He gloated about his stolen uniform, his papers, and the rented apartment.

As soon as she heard the confession, the non-Jewish hostess called over her young son and handed him money so he could run to the store for bread. Inside the rolled-up money was a note for the Nazis. It contained the location of the apartment where the Jews were living. At 3:00 AM, the Nazis burst in with clubs drawn. Anyu leapt to her feet. A Nazi grabbed her from behind, holding her wrists as his counterparts beat the boyfriend senseless. The other Nazis then approached Anyu and slapped her across the face. They demanded to know who she was and where she was from. "A refugee from Transylvania," she pleaded.

"Bullshit," a Nazi shouted back.

Lying was no use; the boyfriend had already told them Anyu was Jewish. The Nazis forced them onto the street and into a large holding car. They stuck a gun to Anyu's stomach and demanded she tell them where her friends were. Anyu said she didn't know. She was telling the truth this time. It was common for Jews on the street never to tell each other where they were hiding. That way, with a gun to their stomach or a blade to their neck, they wouldn't have information to share.

The police station they were brought to consisted of two connected rooms, one for women and one for men. Once a day, Anyu and the rest of the prisoners were given a bowl of soup and a slice of bread. The bread was stiff and dry. The soup was made of caraway seeds. Anyu named it "jailhouse soup." She was so desperate for food that she still insists it was the best soup she's ever had.

She spent a week in jail before being transferred to the Budapest Ghetto. The ghetto had been established a month prior to cage the remaining Jews in Budapest. During Anyu's week-long imprisonment, two boys each day were taken from the jail by the Hungarian soldiers. "To work for the Germans," they said.

Anyu became friends with two Jewish boys in jail, Robby and Geza, who were taken away without warning and never brought back. After the War, Anyu reconnected with Geza, who'd also survived the Holocaust. He shared with her what the Nazis had done that night.

He told her the Nazis had carried him and Robby straight to the Danube River, where only the constant motion of the water prevented it from freezing. The Nazis tied the boys' wrists together and shot Robby in the head. They shoved them both into the river and let Geza sink with his dead friend's corpse.

Geza was able to wrestle himself free of his friend's body and swim to the other side of the riverbank. When he emerged, his teeth were chattering so violently that he put his hands in his mouth so no one would hear. The Nazis were still on the other side of the river, smoking cigarettes. He crawled to the nearest house, shaking, and knocked on the door. The inhabitants were gentiles. They hurried him in and gave him food and dry clothes. But they didn't let him stay. "Who can blame them?" Anyu says.

After the War, Geza moved back to his hometown in Romania, where he became a security agent for the communist government. His job was to hunt for Nazis. Anyu would learn his story long after surviving the Budapest Ghetto. Luckily, unbeknownst to Anyu, Raoul Wallenberg was still in Budapest at the time of her internment in the ghetto. His presence in the city, however, was offset by one of history's most notorious Nazis, Adolf Eichmann, who was also in Budapest. As a mastermind of the Holocaust, Eichmann was committed to the extermination of Budapest's Jews, including Anyu.

chapter 5

seeds & the Farm

I WAS YOUNG TO FALL IN LOVE, BUT I KNEW TRUE beauty when I saw it. Palm trees. Flowing fountains. Spanish architecture. An interdenominational church stood tall in the center of the quad as tourists from around the world posed for pictures under its swooping columns, with bright blues, purples, and golds popping off the tile mural on the church's external façade, depicting timeless scenes from the Old Testament. Laughter zipped through the redwood trees. The grass was freshly trimmed. The air smelled like cedar.

I could get used to Stanford.

My family had made the trip to the Bay Area to visit Anyu. One morning, after fighting a losing battle with *faschilt, ciorba, meggyleves, piros krumpli,* and *almas pite* the night before, we drove the 30 minutes to campus so my sister, who'd just started looking at colleges, could take a tour. As we walked the sunny libraries and stately lecture halls, she was impressed. It was me — the 12-year-old tagalong wearing dirty sneakers and baggy shorts, chatting up the smiling students and asking where the basketball players lived — that was obsessed.

No one in New Jersey ever talked about Stanford. How was that possible? One of the best schools in the world and a top-five basketball team? I could get behind that. Sunshine at all times and no humidity, like, ever? Go on. A half-hour drive from Anyu's apartment, where Hungarian food fell from the sky like raindrops from heaven? Sold.

I was only in seventh grade, still months away from having my Torah portion pounded into my head by my Bar Mitzvah tutor, but despite my early age, Stanford became my dream school. I decided this was where I'd play college basketball. It was true that slow Jewish kids rarely received basketball scholarships from elite programs, but I tried not to get bogged down in the details.

From that day forward, when people asked where I wanted to go to college, I told them Stanford, the best school in the world, right around the corner from my grandmother, the best person in the world. When I talked about my desire to play for the Cardinal, I'd often hear: "Good for you!" or "Wouldn't that be nice?" I'd never smile. My grandma went through hell so I could have opportunities like this. So did my dad, for that matter. I was dead serious about it.

It was at a summer basketball tournament in Los Angeles where I had my first chance to impress Stanford. I'd moved from New Jersey to Milwaukee shortly after my dad was fired by the Knicks. He was now the general manager of the Milwaukee Bucks, the organization with whom he'd started his NBA career. The Bucks had scooped him up as their GM upon his departure from New York. Not only had he built an NBA Finals team, but he'd taken the high road as a media firestorm raged. People had noticed. He was no longer simply an immigrant New Yorker who'd made good in the big city. He was now a top NBA executive with plenty of options outside of the five boroughs.

During my first few weeks living in Milwaukee, as a sophomore in high school without any friends, I spent my nights alone in my room researching card tricks on the Internet and practicing them on my bed. I'd inject some excitement into the evening by working on my shuffling in between tricks. I'd sporadically use the bathroom and make a funny face at myself in the mirror when I walked in, just to have some social interaction with another person my age. I guess moving to Milwaukee can have that type of effect on a kid.

Most of the time, I was thinking about basketball. It wasn't because I loved the game, which I did, but it was because I knew the game could help me prove myself. It was unhealthy how often I thought about becoming a standout basketball player like my dad. It was unhealthy how hard I began to push myself to make it happen.

It wasn't long before I started to enjoy Milwaukee, realizing that the people were far nicer than in New Jersey and that my high school community was far more diverse. I attended one of Wisconsin's top public high schools and started on my varsity basketball team as a sophomore. I was the only white guy in the starting lineup and certainly the only Jewish guy. I'd hit a growth spurt that summer, so my game was now respectable. At 6'2" and 165 pounds, I was a tall tangle of arms and legs. Still skinny and pale but occasionally useful on the court, my primary asset was my shooting ability.

The first colleges to recruit me were small schools in the Midwest. Places like Drake and Illinois State. I got no attention whatsoever from top programs, including Stanford. Whenever I felt discouraged about being lightly recruited, my dad told me to keep working. It was the typical immigrant mentality. "If you work hard," he'd say, "good things will happen."

Athletes at Stanford had to be admitted academically to get a scholarship, so my summer coach repeatedly contacted the Stanford staff to tell them about my strong grades. I wasn't at their level as a player — the Cardinal had been to the Final Four of the NCAA Tournament two years prior and had just won back-to-back conference championships — but I could get in, he'd say, so I was worth a look.

I'd swooned at the Stanford staff from afar at a few of our summer tournaments, always wearing Cardinal red sweater vests with immaculate white polo shirts underneath. They'd never stopped to watch one of my games, but in Los Angeles, for whatever reason, they were willing to take a look. What they saw was a snapshot of post-Bar-Mitzvah adolescence: a 16-year-old Jewish kid with gangly limbs, size-14 feet, smatterings of acne, no muscles, and two very bald underarms. As a player, I could score the basketball fairly well but not nearly as well as my dad. I knew college coaches would compare me to him, unfavorably. He'd been a high school All-American and one of the top recruits in the country. I was nothing in the world of basketball, just a stressed-out kid chasing a ghost.

Before the game in L.A., my coach let me know Stanford had agreed to come watch me play. *Holy crap*, I thought. *Don't overthink it. Just be yourself. Just relax.* By halftime, I had 0 points.

I hadn't spotted Stanford in the crowd, but I was sure I'd ruined my chances with them. Free from pressure, I scored five baskets in a row to start the third quarter. Boom, boom, boom, boom, boom. I ended my third-quarter scoring spree with my first ever in-game dunk. I carefully set up my jump and barely got the ball over the rim, so while the dunk was unremarkable in every way, it was a dunk, nonetheless. "You see Stanford?" my coach said after the game.

"I saw one of the coaches during the third quarter," I said.

"That's when he showed up," my coach said. "He missed the first half."

I paused. Stanford came right before I started my scoring run. Sometimes, it's better to be lucky than good. When I got home to Milwaukee, the recruiting letters from the Cardinal had already started hitting the mailbox. My dad told me he had a good feeling about Stanford. "Why not?" he'd say. "Just keep working."

My next chance was the following summer, when I was invited to the premiere showcase in the nation for high school basketball players. It was called ABCD Camp and it was held in New Jersey, a short drive from where I grew up. Out of hundreds of thousands of high school basketball players in America, only a few hundred got an invitation to this camp. If I could stand out against elite competition

— LeBron James was the camp's best player — Stanford would want me. I set a goal of being named an All-Star at the weeklong event.

Having finished my junior year in high school by then, I'd grown to 6'5" and finally had some whiskers under my arms. I'd averaged more than 17 points per game on a good high school team. I'd lost 80 percent of my acne and gained 20 percent more muscle. I even had a jaw now. When we went to temple on the High Holidays, I wore a tallit, a Jewish prayer shawl used by men, not boys. It stretched comfortably over my thickening shoulders. We attended a seder on Passover, where I no longer asked the Four Questions, a ritual reserved for the youngest person at the table. If given the opportunity, I'd speak openly about my family's experience during the Holocaust. I was still more boy than man, but the proportions were shifting.

By that point, I was one of Stanford's top recruits. I was somehow in striking distance of my seventh-grade promise. I'd even heard a few college coaches say that I played a little like my dad, which I took as a sign that I was on the right track. Anyu's voice shook when we talked about the possibility of Stanford. She'd go on and on and on about all the meats and soups and pastries she'd make me — as if I didn't want Stanford bad enough already.

Every college coach and major sports media outlet in America attended ABCD Camp. Plenty of NBA personnel were there, too, so my dad blended in with his peers as he watched me play. When the games started at camp, I created a nice buzz for myself. I wasn't dominant by any means — LeBron handled those duties, and quite proficiently, I might add — but I was solid and effective. After a few days, several tri-state area newspapers ran stories about me. It was partly due to my play and partly due to my name. It would always be that way. Feature articles about me were written in the *New York Post*, the *New York Daily News*, and *The Bergen Record*, the same papers I'd cut NBA box scores out of as a kid. In one of the articles, I was quoted as referring to my style of play as "cerebral."

What a turd.

Part of me was aware that the attention I was getting wasn't completely my own, but still, I loved it. I couldn't help but wonder if those who'd been so cruel to my dad when he was with the Knicks were reading about my success in New York papers. I thought they might remember the young kid whose life they'd helped upend. They probably did, and they probably didn't give it a second thought. It was me carrying around that negativity, not anyone else. I was the one feeling the pressure and anxiety. I was the one drinking poison and expecting an enemy to suffer its effects.

By the final morning of camp, Stanford was still evaluating me, but I had two games left to impress them. Before the penultimate game started, they announced the All-Star teams — the All-Star game was to be played that night to end camp — and I wasn't on the list. I poured over the names of the All-Stars. *That guy made it?* I'd say to myself as my eyes scanned downward. *That guy made it? That guy made it?* My temples throbbed. I felt like I'd been screwed.

In this case, the anger I was feeling wasn't poison. It was fuel. In the morning game, I scored 20 points, my highest total of camp. In the afternoon game — my last chance to sway Stanford my way and possibly get added to the All-Star team — I had 28 points. It was the first time all week that I'd been the best player on the court. I walked off the floor with a soaked jersey and a satisfied smile. I had a few future NBA players on my team, but I'd been the one with the hot hand. The Cardinal and everyone else now knew I deserved to be an All-Star. Other players at camp started saying I'd be added to the team before the game. At first, I shrugged it off. After a while, I started to believe it.

As I sat in the stands in jeans and a T-shirt that night, my hopes of participating in the All-Star game had sadly disappeared. That was when a voice bellowed over the PA system in the gym: "Dan Grunfeld, please report to the scorer's table."

Whoa! I thought. *Is this really happening?*

Heads turned to look at me. My stomach tingled. "I told you they'd add you," my teammate from camp said, patting me on the back as I got up and made my way down the bleachers.

My heart was already pounding. The scorer's table was on the other side of the gym, but I didn't mind my lengthy strut over there. I was going to enjoy this walk. I'd earned this. *How could Stanford resist me now? What number would my All-Star jersey be? Would I play with LeBron or against him?*

When I strolled up to the scorer's table, I expected a congratulations, a round of applause, and a newly printed All-Star jersey. I would have welcomed a marching band, but it wasn't a requirement. Once I got to my destination, the guy in charge of the PA system barely looked at me. "Hey Grunfeld, this lady is here to see you," he said.

This lady? That was not what I wanted to hear. I wasn't expecting any visitors. I was expecting to be added to the All-Star team, to impress Stanford, to play on the same court as LeBron James. I was expecting validation, damn it.

Instead, my head spun like a dreidel as I was greeted by the grinning face of Mrs. Brandeis, the 4'10" Hebrew school tutor who'd prepared me for my Bar Mitzvah. I hadn't spoken to her since I'd ascended the bimah as an awkward 13 year old, but she'd seen the article about me in the local newspaper and, bless her, had tracked me down to this gymnasium like the miniature Mossad agent that she was.

When I made contact with her tiny oval eyes, I tried to shake this nightmare away. I let out an ironic laugh, though I was, of course, crying on the inside. Mrs. Brandeis hadn't just stopped by to say hello. She was holding a gift bag for me adorned with a big red bow. She handed it to me and gave me a kiss on the cheek in front of everyone. Players, coaches, media, LeBron, everyone. I peeked inside the baggie and saw a small black T-shirt on top that would've fit the unripe version of me that she used to tutor. The back of my neck burned. The good Jewish boy my mother raised tried to be gracious, but the 17-year-old high school basketball player trying to build a reputation overrode that and wanted the moment to end immediately, by any means necessary.

I stood and chatted with my Bar Mitzvah tutor for a few minutes before excusing myself. I looked around the packed gym and could feel my face turning different shades of maroon. I carried my dynamite gift bag back to the stands. At that point, I wished it were actually filled with dynamite.

I ended up not staying to watch the All-Star game. A childhood friend picked me up from the gym so we could hang out at his house. I threw the gift bag in his closet when we got home. It likely remains there to this day.

My last chance to get to Stanford was a few weeks later in Las Vegas, at the biggest national tournament of the summer. I'd be competing with my AAU team, a collection of top players from the city of Milwaukee. Once again, I'd have the opportunity to measure up to guys like LeBron. With four years with Anyu on the line, these were the most important basketball games of my life.

When I walked into the gym for the first game of the tournament, the stands were lined with college coaches. Right in the center, in Cardinal red sweater vests and white polo shirts, was the Stanford staff. They were there for me.

On the first play of that first game, I shot the ball as soon as I touched it. This was unlike me, since I usually spent a few minutes settling into the flow of the game before asserting myself. Something was different now. Without even thinking, I'd shot a deep two-pointer with a hand in my face, a low percentage shot I normally wouldn't take. But it went in. And so did the next one. And the next one. And the next one. They were all going in, and I wasn't thinking about any of them. That's probably why they were going in. I'd always overanalyzed the game, worrying about expectations and opinions and legacy. I'm not sure why my brain shut off at such a crucial moment, but I'll never forget that liberation, the feeling of being free from myself — if only for a few hours.

I was a scorer, so I always knew how many points I had during a game. It wasn't something I kept track of but more of a subconscious tally system that most scorers have. That game, I logged no mental data on my performance. I lost myself. In a game that could shape the rest of my life, my mind had been wiped clean.

We ended up losing by two points to a talented team from Washington state. We had a chance to tie it on the last possession, but I didn't get the ball for the final shot. When our attempt rimmed out, I stormed off the court. I'd wanted to take that shot. I was pacing on the sideline, muttering words of frustration to myself, when my assistant coach approached with a smile on his face. "Why the hell are you smiling?" I growled. "We lost."

He grabbed me. "Don't worry about the loss," he said. "Do you know how many points you had?"

My mind clicked back to reality. I thought about his question and realized I'd lost count. The one thing I knew was that I'd been scoring in bunches. Stanford returned to my mind. "Actually, I have no clue," I said. "How many?"

He paused for a second. "You have no idea?"

"None," I said. "I was lost in my own world."

"Whatever happened, it worked," he said, "because you had 45 points."

I stared at him. Neither one of us said anything. I closed my eyes. "Are you fucking serious?" I asked.

I'd never scored that many points in my life. It was a record that year among the 3,000 players in the tournament. LeBron himself didn't score that many. Forty-five points in 32 minutes. Some force in the world, invisible but powerful, wanted me and Anyu together.

I had the best game of my life at the moment I needed it most. As hard as I worked, I didn't will it to happen. I can't really claim credit for it. I just put myself in a position to get lucky. Some of it was due to my preparation, some of it was on the universe for rewarding preparation, but I think the majority of it was because of one great person, Anyu, who'd finally been assigned good karma.

Mike Montgomery, Stanford's head coach, called my hotel room a few days later and offered me a scholarship. I allowed myself a quick smile. I'd be spending four years in California eating *rántott hús*. I'd be playing basketball at a top program at one of the best schools in the world. I'd done what I said I'd do in seventh grade. After a minute, I cleared the smile from my face and pressed the phone closer to my ear.

Obsession is dangerous, since it never ends. New expectations emerge, new goals are set, new horizons appear. My dad had been a top NBA draft pick, and no Jewish player had been drafted as high since. I'd gotten to Stanford, but my need to prove my worth, my obligation to the past, my anger, it all remained. It was just my definition of success that had changed. And it had happened almost instantly. As I called Anyu to share the news about Stanford, I was already thinking about what was next. Her shrieks and tears made me forget about everything I needed to become, but just for a minute.

chapter 6

Eichmann & Wallenberg

A DOLF EICHMANN'S THIN EYES CONVEYED HIS obsession with efficiency. He was a master of logistics, an operational specialist, the literal devil in the details. He's been called the architect of the Holocaust. It was Eichmann who planned the complex processes through which Jews were rounded up across Europe and transported to killing centers. Identification, assembly, transportation, annihilation. Eichmann presided over the Nazis' entire death funnel.

Before World War II, Eichmann had been an unremarkable student, floating from day laborer to office worker to traveling salesman for the Vacuum Oil Company. After the War, he justified his role in the murder of millions by repeating his claim that he was merely following orders.

In late 1944, when Anyu was taken from the Nazi jail to the Budapest Ghetto, which contained 80,000 Jews packed into a few city blocks, Eichmann was already in Budapest. He'd arrived the day the Nazis invaded. Usually, others around the globe implemented his plans as he coordinated from afar. It was only in Hungary that Eichmann was on the ground. He'd toured Chelmno and Auschwitz, but he'd never involved himself directly in the deportation of Jews, until now. The Russians were gaining ground, so his presence was required.

Anyu arrived in the ghetto in December. The trees were bare, and the dirt had frozen over. She was wearing her only possessions: battered shoes, a thin cotton dress, and a dirty winter coat. It took Anyu a few days in the ghetto to get her bearings. It was surrounded by a high fence and a stone wall, with Nazi guards patrolling the perimeter. Nothing was allowed in and nothing was allowed out.

Garbage and waste piled up with no method of collection. Fresh air evaporated. Typhoid and dysentery spread. Bodies lined the streets. Buildings were filled with the dead. The smell carried.

Jewish ghettos were common during World War II. They were established across Europe to segregate Jews from the general population. The most notorious ghetto was in Warsaw, Poland. More than 400,000 Jews occupied the ghetto's 1.3 square miles. When the Russians liberated Warsaw in 1945, there were 175,000 total people left in the city, 6 percent of the pre-war population, and only 11,500 of them were Jews.

The majority of inhabitants in Jewish ghettos died from disease or were starved, shot, or deported to death camps. Nazi-appointed Jewish councils were tasked with administering daily life in the ghetto. Ghetto police forces were established to carry out the Nazis' orders. Jobs were distributed to able-bodied prisoners. Anyu's job was as a nurse, caring for the sick and dying. She had no medicine or training. The patients had no beds and were laid out on the floor. Anyu tried to do her best.

With the Russians and the Germans fighting for control of Budapest, bomb blasts and gunshots became white noise. Effective hiding was done in basements. The air in these confined spaces was stiff and freezing. Anyu's coat was her only protection. Bread was distributed sparingly. Anyu had found some mustard in an empty apartment building in the ghetto, and she hid it in her coat pocket. It was gold. She rationed wisely. The pungent burn tickled her tongue. Her taste buds prickled, and she thought of *libamáj*, homemade *foie gras* made from goose liver. She'd taken her mother's cooking for granted. Those familiar tastes now seemed to belong to a different world.

There was a faucet on the street that sometimes had water. When the bullets slowed and the bombs ceased, Anyu would steal a few sips. She'd be back underground before her lips dried.

Anyu talked to other prisoners whenever possible to get information. She had no idea what had happened to her family and neither did anyone else. A man she met in the ghetto named Kaufman, her mother's maiden name, turned out to be her third cousin on her father's side, where there were also Kaufmans. He had no information, but he was wearing two pairs of pants. He gave Anyu one of them. Young women in Europe wore dresses back then, so this was the first pair of pants she'd ever put on. The act of kindness brought her to tears. The cracked skin on her legs began to soften.

One afternoon in the ghetto, a boy approached Anyu. His hair was greasy and his shirt torn at the neck. He looked new to this place, clearly disoriented. Anyu asked where he'd been. When the boy disclosed the number of a labor camp in Hungary, Anyu's eyes widened. "I had a brother in that camp," she said in Hungarian. "Andy Samuel. Did you know him?"

Now, the boy's eyes widened. "I know Andy," he said. "He's a few streets over."

The whole labor camp had been moved to the ghetto as the Russians advanced. Anyu's brother was not only alive, he was also nearby. Anyu smiled for the first time in weeks. She asked someone to watch over her patients and bolted into the street. The gunfire made her jump. Her heart raced, a combination of fear and excitement. She backed into the doorway, caught her breath, and waited for the fighting to subside. She couldn't see the guns, but she could hear them.

Pop. Pop. Pop.

Eventually, silence. She ran to the next building.

When the gunfire picked up, she ducked inside again. She bent in and out of houses until she reached the area the boy had spoken of. One boy led to another boy who led to her brother. Things were too grave to celebrate, but Anyu threw her arms around Andy and kissed his cheeks. He was skinny and dirty. So was she. Anyu held Andy's hand as they weaved their way back to the building where Anyu had been staying. They decided they'd hunker there together. Andy found an old mattress that he and Anyu slept on. Their sister Shari was in the ghetto, too, Anyu had learned. She had a spot on the floor for herself in a separate building. She didn't want to give it up, since space was precious. Anyu and Andy visited when they could.

By early January 1945, German control in Budapest had weakened, and it appeared that the War would soon be over. Then one day, Anyu saw Nazis gathering at the front gate of the ghetto. They had machine guns on their shoulders. She froze.

The Nazis usually stayed out of the ghetto. Now, there were bunches of them, and they were being organized into groups. There was nothing more threatening than the enemy in formation. Word quickly spread that the Nazis were there to liquidate the ghetto. All 80,000 remaining Jews were to be massacred. It was a direct order from Adolf Eichmann.

Upon seeing the Nazis, Andy grabbed Anyu's arm and pulled her to their building's stairs. Their weak legs propelled them up flight after flight until there was no place left to go. Breathless, they reached an attic and shuffled inside an interior closet space. It was big enough for four or five people. Andy put his finger to his mouth, signaling to Anyu to stay quiet.

They quickly heard footsteps pounding up the stairs behind them, but it wasn't the Nazis. It was more terrified Jews. A dozen or so joined them in the attic. The group was well concealed, but not an inch remained. They hushed their breathing and stayed as still as possible. Anyu felt Andy's shoulder on hers. She closed her eyes and listened for signs of the Nazis from the street below. Yelling, screaming, gunshots, anything. Anyu could feel hot breath on her cold neck. She waited. They waited. The silence persisted. They stood motionless in the attic for five minutes. Then 20. Then an hour.

Whispers started. "We'd have heard something by now, right?"

Ten more minutes. The whispers intensified. "What should we do?"

As a group, they decided they needed to check. One person would have to look out a window onto the ghetto to see what was happening. Not to disrupt the cramped space, they chose the boy closest to the exit, who had no choice but to obey. He crept down the stairs to the nearest window with a view of the ghetto's entrance. Nothing. The boy craned his neck and glanced in all directions. It was true. The Nazis were gone. The ghetto was clear. The boy hurried back to the attic and shared the report. Anyu exhaled for the first time in hours. Months, really. She was sure she'd have been dead by now.

They filed out of the attic as Russian and Romanian soldiers arrived in the ghetto. They were told that the Nazis had retreated. The Budapest Ghetto had been liberated, and they were free to go home. No one would try to kill them anymore.

It was January 18, 1945. Anyu, Shari, and Andy left the ghetto together. They were once again able to feel strength in numbers. They had no idea why the Nazis with the machine guns had disappeared. At that point, they weren't thinking much about it. They found some thread after leaving the ghetto and traded it for scraps of food. They splashed water on their faces. They managed to laugh.

Anyu's brother was soon taken prisoner by the Russians, escaping not long after by altering his identification to make himself seem too young for labor. Anyu and Shari stayed together in a small room in a Budapest building for a few weeks after liberation. By then, Russian soldiers were raping freed Jewish girls at a dizzying pace. Anyu — 19, blonde, and attractive — hid from them whenever they were near. In a world gone mad, even the good guys were bad.

Anyu decided to make the journey back to Micula. At the train station, there was no schedule or order. There were barely any trains — just a mass of people who'd come to be known as Holocaust survivors trying to go home to get some damn rest. Anyu sat and waited. After half a day, she got on a train with her sister to Debrecen, Hungary, where their mother's sister lived. During the overnight passage, a drunk Russian soldier was lumbering up the aisle of the train car, striking a match and holding it up to the faces of young female passengers. He was assessing the inventory. Anyu kept her eyes averted until she smelled his drunk breath and felt the heat of the match's light tinge her face. She jerked her head up. Acting on instinct, she locked her eyes with his and blew out his match with a forceful puff. Bullies can sense who should and should not be bothered. The soldier continued up the aisle.

When Anyu finally arrived at her aunt's house, no one was there. Luckily, her aunt would soon return. She'd survived World War II in Austria, where she was forced to serve as the housemaid of an SS officer on the Austrian front. Anyu caught a train back to Satu Mare, then to Micula. She was almost home. She thought of her mother and father and siblings and hoped they were okay. The nightmare seemed to be over, but really it was just beginning. She had no indication of what had happened to her family or to six million other Jews. She'd have a lifetime to try to make sense of it all. It still hasn't been enough.

It was 15 years later when the Israelis found Adolf Eichmann. He'd escaped Hungary after the War using false documents and had settled in the north of Germany under an assumed name. With the help of Nazi-sympathizing Catholic Church officials, Eichmann obtained more fake identification that allowed him to flee to Argentina. He sent for his family and lived in Buenos Aires, working small jobs before becoming a department head with Mercedes-Benz. By then, he was known as Ricardo Klement.

Jews across the globe kept hunting Eichmann. They craved justice for what he'd done. Through information aggregated from dozens of sources, including famed Nazi-hunter Simon Wiesenthal, the Israelis located Eichmann in Buenos Aires. Israeli Mossad agents grabbed him one evening after he stepped off the bus from work. They took him to a safe house and confirmed his identity. Accomplished without authorization from the government of Argentina, the elaborate mission was clandestine. Israel knew it was violating Argentina's sovereignty, but that was a small price to pay to get Eichmann. Documents would later show that the CIA, the Central Intelligence Agency of the United States, knew Eichmann was in Argentina for several years before his capture. They didn't act to bring him to justice because it didn't serve American interests in the Cold War.

The Israelis drugged Eichmann and dressed him as a flight attendant for Israel's national airline. This time, the Jews provided the false identification for Eichmann. They boarded him onto a commercial plane bound for the Holy Land. On May 22, 1960, Adolf Eichmann landed in Israel. He'd flown El Al. Eichmann stood trial in Jerusalem. His actions in Budapest — his death march, his last-minute attempt to exterminate the Jews in the ghetto — were a focal point of his prosecution. He was hanged outside Tel Aviv, the only person ever executed by the State of Israel. His ashes were spread in the sea beyond Israeli waters. He claimed until the end that he was just following orders.

Hannah Arendt's *Eichmann in Jerusalem* famously captures the trial and analyzes the man. Into her 90s, Anyu would read a Hungarian copy of the book with her feet up on the couch in her beautiful Bay Area apartment. She'd read its haunting details a dozen times prior. She'd never gotten pleasure from reading the book, but she read it nonetheless, over and over.

In 1985, four decades after the liberation of the Budapest Ghetto, *Wallenberg: A Hero's Story* was released as a made-for-TV movie. Richard Chamberlain played the title character, Raoul Wallenberg, who'd disappeared in Budapest after the War. He was believed to have been captured and killed by the Soviets. He'd saved 100,000 Jewish lives. Anyu had the date of the TV premiere circled on her calendar. She'd always told friends that Wallenberg had saved her life during the War. His Schutz-Pass gave her security. His existence gave her hope.

As she watched the movie with my grandpa, scenes unfolded that she could replay from memory: the invasion of Hungary, the distribution of the Schutz-Passes, the formation of the ghetto, Eichmann's presence in Budapest, the arrival of the Russians. Near the end of the film, Nazis storm into the Budapest Ghetto with machine guns. They had orders from Eichmann to murder all remaining Jews. The frame jumps to a frantic Wallenberg driving a car, furiously trying to reach the ghetto. He barely puts his car in park as he jumps out and locates General Gerhard Schmidhuber, commander of the German troops in Hungary. He was the man instructed to carry out the massacre and the only man who had the authority to stop it.

Playing the main character, Richard Chamberlain pleads with the general. He begs him to spare these peoples' lives. He lets him know that the War is over and that he will hang for what he's about to do. That convinces the general to call off the massacre. The Nazis with machine guns are ordered out of the ghetto. They walk through the front gate and never return. The ghetto is soon liberated. It had taken Anyu 40 years to find out why the Nazis disappeared after her hours spent hiding in the attic that day. She now tells her friends that Raoul Wallenberg saved her life not once but twice during the War.

When Anyu and I visited the Holocaust Museum in Washington, D.C. together for the first time, there was one small section of the museum she was focused on showing me. Most people wouldn't stop there, she said, but it was important to her that I knew it existed. Anyu held my hand as we walked through the museum. We were mostly quiet as we passed the photo exhibits of Auschwitz and the memorial to the Budapest Ghetto. We'd pause for a minute, take it in, and move on. We passed a wall with city names in Transylvania where Jews were lost. We found Micula. We passed a variety of exhibits — on the crematoria, on the international response, on the timeline for the Final Solution — until we arrived at our destination.

Anyu squeezed my hand and looked at me. She was wearing a silk scarf, her silver hair shining. She pointed at his face and made me promise I'd remember him. She made me promise that when I had kids, they'd know about him, too. I nodded my head and began to read the block of text under Wallenberg's photo.

chapter 7

a tic & the clock

ANYU CAME TO EVERY HOME GAME I PLAYED AT STANFORD. I'd leave two tickets for her at the entrance to the arena so she could bring her friend Lily Spitz with her. They'd known each other since before the War, since before Anyu survived the streets of Budapest and Lily Spitz came home from Auschwitz.

Anyu picked Lily up before each game and drove the half hour to Stanford's campus. She was a surprisingly strong driver considering she used her right foot to operate the gas and her left foot to operate the brake, an absolutely baffling driving technique. She didn't learn to drive until her 40s, but I'm not sure that can explain it. I've never seen anyone else drive like that. As with most things, Anyu made it look easy. In all her years on the road, she never had a car accident.

The other guests who packed Stanford's family section for our games would hear a foreign language sprinkled into the crowd's rumblings, but they knew nothing about its origins. Anyu never mentioned the details of her background, and Lily's sleeve covered the tattoo on her left forearm. Her identification number at Auschwitz — A-10785 — followed her everywhere.

Anyu had been watching basketball for decades, but she didn't comment or critique or yell at the refs like others in the family section. She just sat and observed, silently *kvelling* whenever I took the court for the Cardinal. She wore silk blouses, red lipstick, and enough Aqua Net hairspray to burn a small hole into the ozone layer. Win or lose, I'd usually keep a few teammates waiting after games as I walked with Anyu to her car to pick up the food she'd brought me. She'd be at my dorm a few days later to drop off my laundry and stock the fridge — always with a steaming container of fried matzo for me, always wrapped in a towel so it stayed hot — but even so, she couldn't miss an opportunity to send me home with something to eat.

I'd finished high school as one of the top 100 basketball players in the nation, and though I was promising as a freshman at Stanford, I'd never had an experience like my sophomore year, when I played on the No. 1-ranked college basketball team in the country. We started that season by winning 26 games in a row. We beat No. 1 Kansas to become 4-0 and No. 3 Arizona to get to 13-0. We hit a three-pointer at the buzzer against Arizona to win our 20th straight and a three-pointer at the buzzer against Washington State to win our 26th straight.

We were the most dominant team in college basketball, and we only had one future NBA player. All five of Arizona's starters played in the NBA. We'd managed to make ourselves unbeatable through a perfect combination of skill, toughness, discipline, unselfishness, and luck. Because of our late-game heroics and incredible winning streak, we'd become college basketball's golden boys.

I'd dreamt for years about slipping my own Stanford jersey over my shoulders. Now, I had a No. 20 in cardinal and white with my name on it. I'd picked 20 because my dad had worn it in the NBA. By some miracle, I'd gone from a basketball-obsessed string bean to part of Stanford's top-ranked team. If that weren't enough, that team was a national sensation and a true feel-good story for sports fans across the country.

There was just one person who wasn't feeling good about it: me.

I was an embarrassment as a college basketball player. I was the worst player on my No. 1-ranked team — by far. I also believe I was the worst player in the Pac-10 Conference. I couldn't have begged another program to take me. For someone on the best team in the country to be the worst player in the conference seems impossible, but with the depths of my futility, nothing was impossible. I had horrible shooting percentages, a paltry scoring average, and dwindling minutes over the course of the season. I couldn't deal with getting fewer shots than I thought I deserved. I couldn't deal with being a marginal player, even on a great team. My ambition far outpaced my opportunity. It probably outpaced my ability, too.

Off the court, Stanford was everything I'd hoped for and more. I partied and laughed and made lifelong friends. Basketball was just the one slice of my life that was filled with tension. It eventually consumed everything I was doing. I wanted to be special so fucking bad.

My dad had finished his sophomore season in college averaging 23.8 points per game. That was the benchmark others would measure me against. I'd finish my sophomore season averaging 3.4. During games, my mind would race, a relentless loop of criticism, doubt, and judgement. I felt no space to play the game freely and naturally, the way it needs to be played. All I could do was think about myself and my story. It was always about me.

The anxiety was so pervasive that I asked my mom if I should start medicating myself before games. I decided not to because I had too much anxiety about inadvertently failing a drug test from medicating myself. For the record, I'd never once been given a drug test at Stanford. That thought process is simply a glimpse into the mind of someone who was spiraling.

When I struggled on the court, my insecurities surfaced. I felt as if everyone watching me thought that I didn't deserve to be where I was, that I was flying high on borrowed wings, that I was a joke. I'm sure part of me worried that everyone was right. I was fighting against a lot — past injustice, current perception, the future of a legacy — and sometimes it just felt like too much to carry.

Anyu's advice was not to take it to my heart. She told me that she was proud of me and that everything would be okay. Dad assured me that good things would happen if I just kept working. He told me to try to focus on the team's success. He never put pressure on me to excel at basketball, and I had the best mom and sister in the world. All my issues were self-imposed.

Even with the massive amount of support from my family, I didn't have whatever I needed. I couldn't cope with performing so poorly and so publicly. I wanted to feel better and my loved ones wanted me to feel better. I just wasn't capable of it.

By the end of the season, the nervous tic I'd had as a kid returned. My eyes would tighten from stress, and the only way to relieve the tension would be to shift them from side to side and blink repeatedly. My breathing shortened when I thought about the tic. It controlled me. The powerlessness only made it worse. Any time I was at the free-throw line during a game, all I could think about was how obvious it must be.

I'm ashamed to say that I wanted the season to end. If that sounds selfish, it's because it was. We had a chance to win the national championship, but I was suffering. I was too immature to prioritize anyone other than myself.

We entered the NCAA Tournament as the No. 1 seed in the West Region. My parents and sister flew from Washington, D.C. to Spokane, Washington to watch us play. In the first round, we beat the University of Texas-San Antonio by 26. I played 13 minutes and scored four points. My parents sat with me on a couch in the hotel lobby after the game. They tried to calm me down. Relax and enjoy the ride, they said. They reminded me that I'd always wanted to play for Stanford, that I was only a sophomore, and that I was getting minutes on the top team in the country. I was blinking uncontrollably.

Our second-round game was against Alabama, the No. 8 seed in our bracket. Our Stanford team was the most focused and committed I've played on — we had voluntary workouts at 7:00 AM the summer before the season, and if anyone was a minute late, we'd meet at 6:00 AM the next day, which only happened once. For whatever reason, though, we could never separate from Alabama. We were 30-1 up to that point. We just had an off day at the wrong time. After a back-and-forth contest, we found ourselves down 70-67 with a few seconds remaining. Our best player, Josh Childress, had fouled out in the final seconds, and I was subbed in to replace him. When Coach called my name, I popped off the bench without thinking and ran to the scorer's table. I had a deep pit in my stomach. I'd only played seven minutes all game and had no points, one assist, and four fouls.

As I jogged onto the court, an Alabama player was going to the line. All he needed to do was make one of two free throws and the game would be over. The packed arena was teeming with the nervous energy that builds before a massive upset. The lower bowl was a sea of red, with our fans in cardinal and their fans in crimson. Our side was dazed, unable to believe what was happening. Their side was delirious. Alabama, an average team in the SEC, was about to beat Stanford, the Pac-10 champions who'd only lost once all year.

I'd wanted the season to end, but not like this. I stood in rebounding position at the free-throw line and glanced around. My teammates' faces were blank. With one make, we'd become a footnote in history, another top seed that couldn't get it done when it mattered.

When the first free throw banged off the rim, we had a glimmer of hope. There were only a few seconds left, but another miss would give us a chance to rush the ball up court for a game-tying three-pointer. Waiting for the second free throw, I shifted back and forth to get the blood flowing through my legs. I'd been sitting on the bench for most of the half. As the second shot was released, my legs felt like soggy bread. I traced the ball's trajectory as it arched into the air and veered slightly off course. The shot fell off the rim and into the hands of one of my teammates. My heart raced. There was no playbook for this type of situation. We had to get the ball up court and shoot a three — by any means necessary.

I dropped my head and started to sprint. My teammate pushed the ball up the floor as the seconds melted off the clock. ...5...4...3... My stiff legs started to activate, carrying me up the right side of the court in a hurry. I had no time to think. All I could do was run.

I have no recollection of the fans at that moment, but I'm sure they were on their feet. If there's one thing human beings love, it's drama. We were a No. 1 seed in the NCAA Tournament with the chance to avoid a huge upset at the buzzer. I used to sneak a transistor radio into class during the NCAA Tournament to listen to finishes like this. My mom used to let me stay home from school for a day during the NCAA Tournament to watch finishes like this.

As the ball crossed half court, time was about to expire. That's when my teammate turned in my direction. Without hesitating, he swung the ball to me on the right wing.

He knew I could shoot — I was one of the best shooters in the country coming out of high school — but I hadn't taken a shot with confidence in months. By the end of the season, I was passing up open looks because I was afraid I'd airball them. It was one of the most important possessions in the history of Stanford's basketball program, and the ball was in my hands. I wasn't wide open, but I had some space, and the horn was about to sound.

Fuck it.

I rose up off the ground, tucking my elbow in and squaring my shoulders just like my dad had shown so many times during those shooting clinics when I was a kid. I snapped my wrist and let the damn thing fly as the buzzer blared through the arena. My mom, dad, and sister were looking on with the others in the family section. Anyu was watching on TV in the Bay Area.

They didn't know it, but the shot felt good when it rolled off my fingertips. I watched the ball float through the air. If it could somehow drop through that metal cylinder, I'd be a hero. All those years of feeling desperate to make people proud would've been leading to this moment. With a single three-pointer, it would've all made sense. Instead, the shot smacked off the side of the rim.

I fell to the ground with my hands on my head as Alabama players jumped in each other's arms around me. I was frozen to the floor. All I could do was try to blink it away. The aftermath of the shot was a blur. The locker room was a blur. The reporters surrounding my locker and sticking their microphones and tape recorders in my face were a blur. The season was over, but there was no reprieve from what I'd been feeling.

As I boarded the team bus after the game, my cell phone rang. It was my dad. "Hey," I answered.

"I love you, man," is how he started.

As a kid, I'd have done anything to be a Stanford Cardinal. In the aftermath of the Alabama game, I was being mocked on ESPN for missing one of the biggest shots in the school's history. I remember exactly how they phrased it as the highlight of the final play ran.

"And the ball swings to...Dan Grunfeld???"

The implication was clear: why is this schmuck taking the final shot?

I knew one of the ESPN anchors on the show, so I emailed him to tell him that they'd be sorry they disrespected me like that. I told him that the following year would be different, that they'd be saying my name differently then. He never wrote me back. He probably thought I was a psycho. He was right.

Everyone was underestimating me, but I stood on the shoulders of those who never had a chance to be great. I stood on the shoulders of someone who'd already done the unimaginable. It seemed ridiculous, but I still believed I could make it to the NBA. If there's one thing you should never underestimate, it's the human heart on fire.

Besides, I had a plan.

chapter 8

gypsies & Transylvania

B EFORE THE 1936 OLYMPICS IN BERLIN, GYPSY families were marched at gunpoint to a sewage disposal site in Marzhan, a Berlin suburb. The Nazi party wanted gypsies kept away from visitors to preserve an image of Germany's purity. At the same time, the city of Berlin was stripped of all anti-Semitic rhetoric. The signs that prohibited Jews from entering public facilities were removed. The anti-Semitic newspaper *Der Sturmer*, with its catchphrase, "The Jews are our misfortune," was temporarily pulled from newsstands. The Olympics proceeded without incident.

It was the first year basketball was played at the Olympic Games. The majority of basketball players at the time were Jewish. According to Paul Gallico, sports editor of the *New York Daily News* in the 1930s, basketball was a particularly Jewish sport because "the game places a premium on an alert, scheming mind, flashy trickiness, artful dodging and general smart aleckness."

The United States defeated Canada to win the first Olympic basketball gold medal in Berlin. The game was played outside, on a dirt court, in the rain. The final score was 19-8. James Naismith, the inventor of the game of basketball, awarded the medals. After the Olympics concluded, the gypsies were kept in Marzhan and the anti-Semitic propaganda returned to German streets. Years later, the gypsies and the Jews were both sent to Auschwitz.

In the early 1960s in Transylvania, on the Romania side of the Romania-Hungary border, the gypsies my dad saw on a daily basis lived in horse-drawn wagons. They were vagabonds, wandering on dusty roads, their clothes torn and their faces tired. They begged for money on the street or played the violin for tips. They developed a cottage industry: knife sharpening. They became experts and went door-to-door offering their services. Gypsies in Romania, like in Germany, were viewed as a substandard people. They were considered outcasts and were not to be trusted. Parents in Romania scared their kids by telling them gypsies stole children who got too close. Dad wasn't afraid of gypsies just because they were different. As a Jew, he was also different. Kids at school had grandparents, but Dad had none. Anyu would occasionally give him a piece of bread with *schmaltz* on it, as a treat. He'd walk out to the road and hand the gypsies the bread. They always needed something to eat, and he had plenty. At least that's what it felt like.

My dad's father worked a typical communist-era job in Transylvania: he managed a state-run store that sold used and distressed materials like ripped fabric, splintered rocking chairs, or broken wheel barrels. The store also carried mismatched pairs of shoes. One shoe in a pair would be black, the other would be brown, or the shoes would be different sizes altogether.

In Communist Romania, there were no bright lights like in Paris or London or New York City. There was only one shade of gray under communism, but life was still somehow beautiful to Dad. He hadn't yet seen in color.

Dad claims he didn't grow up poor. Without TV or the Internet, there was no point of comparison. Communism was merely his norm. He had no idea that kids in other countries had toys, plumbing, and plans. All he knew was that his parents made him feel safe and his big brother took him everywhere. He had friends, food, and a devoted family. It didn't seem like childhood could get any better than that. Like most people in Transylvania, Dad spoke Hungarian and Romanian and had no reason to learn English. He'd heard of a sport called basketball, but he'd never played it before. He'd never even seen it being played. Nothing about his existence could have indicated that he'd one day win a gold medal at the Olympics playing basketball for the United States of America — exactly 40 years after the first basketball gold medals were awarded in Hitler's Germany.

Dad grew up in Satu Mare, a Romanian city on the Someş River and the closest big city to Anyu's hometown village of Micula. During hot summers in the heart of Transylvania, a wet towel on the chest served as air conditioning. In the winter, wood was burned in a small hatch in the apartment. Pickled vegetables were stockpiled to last through the cold. There was no running water inside, so a pump in the courtyard was shared with a dozen families. It was eventually changed to a faucet. Everyone celebrated.

No running water at home meant no indoor bathrooms. As a toddler, Dad would pee and poop into a little bowl, then Anyu would take the contents to the outhouse and dump them down the toilet. That was somehow an improvement from Dad's days in diapers, when Anyu would hand-wash his soiled cloth and flannel coverings each night in a small wooden tub, ironing them once dry so they'd lay soft and smooth on his backside. When Dad was old enough, he accessed the outhouse with a key. The family shared the toilet with a neighbor. There was no shower. For baths, Anyu collected water from the shared tap in a large bucket and heated it on the wood-burning stove. A friend in Satu Mare had a bathtub, and Anyu would sometimes walk Dad the few miles to her house to use it.

In the courtyard, neighbors butchered animals. Chickens ran around with no heads, just for a second. Pigs were killed and chopped into chunks before being carried off to a smokehouse behind an apartment. In winter, after a pig was broken down, the powdery courtyard snow was streaked with ruby red pig's blood. On weekends, Anyu would sit on the ground in the courtyard with a goose in her arms. There'd be a bowl of cornmeal at her feet. She'd hold the goose's neck between her legs, open its jaws, and force the meal down its throat. This practice would enlarge the goose's liver, often to 10 times its normal volume. It was done to ensure a generous offering of *foie gras* upon slaughter. She'd seen her mother force-feed the goose countless times back in Micula, before the War.

Living under a communist regime, Dad didn't have toys, so he used his imagination. When he came across a rope to play with, he'd dangle it behind himself like a snake, slithering it from side to side, hissing it down the street. His friend's dad was a tailor, so when they'd find old boxes, the friend would cut them into armor and a helmet. Cardboard and scissors created kings, knights, and gladiators. And no equipment was needed to play hide and seek or chase frogs by the river.

Mostly, Dad played football, the European kind, alongside kids in his neighborhood. With thick legs and huge hands, he was the biggest of all his friends, and he moved well for his size. There was already evidence of power, coordination, and competitiveness, even though no one was looking for it. To start the game, they'd find a large stone and set it several feet from a curb to create the goal. The old checkered ball would drop, and they'd be off. It was usually three-on-three, no goalies. The games were fast and informal. The older kids played soccer down by the river.

At home, they didn't talk about the Holocaust, but its weight pressed down. The whole world knew that six million Jews had been killed. More than one million of those deaths had happened at Auschwitz. Ninety thousand or so Jews in northern Transylvania had been deported to Auschwitz. Eight hundred thousand Jews had died in ghettos, including in Budapest. Anyu lost 70 close family members, and my grandpa lost everyone. When they went to synagogue on the High Holidays, the catastrophe loomed. Anyu was stiff as she remembered her loved ones. She thought of her father. How he was lost could not be forgotten. All the death was never front and center but always present. A lifetime isn't enough to erase the shadow of Auschwitz. Its smudge will persist through human history, the ultimate reminder of what we're capable of.

After the Holocaust, tragedy was tucked away, and normalcy became the goal. Anyu and Apu joined a local club during summer so the family could swim in the river. Dad took accordion and French lessons. Apu brought Dad to any sporting event he could find, mostly Dinamo Satu Mare soccer games but also local Ping-Pong or volleyball matches. In Bucharest, Apu bought a tape recorder and one of the most popular records of the day. They didn't have these luxuries in Satu Mare, so Anyu played the song on repeat. Even communism could be neutralized by the bounce of an upbeat tune. Feet tapped as the creamy voice of Harry Belafonte — a New Yorker of Jamaican descent with a Dutch-Jewish grandfather — blared from the tape recorder:

"Come mister tally man, tally me banana
Daylight come and me wan' go home."

At the town's small movie theater, Dad saw *Moby Dick* three times. His eyes spent hours locked on the screen. He'd never before been exposed to such a magnificent spectacle. The sea, the whale, the film — they were all bigger than life. As soon as *Moby Dick* ended, his only thought was when he could see it again. The movie was in English with Romanian subtitles. He didn't speak English and couldn't read Romanian.

On a trip to the Black Sea as a young boy, Dad saw an African man for the first time. He'd never seen someone with Black skin before. He asked his dad about it. Apu's response was that people are just people. Judge everyone as an individual and always get to know someone before forming an opinion. Don't make assumptions. If anyone should know that, it was the Jews. Anyu and Apu had been discriminated against before and wouldn't dare discriminate against others. They didn't have a proper academic education, but they'd been well educated in the school of life. Fairness was the pillar of that curriculum.

Anyu tried her best to recreate the happy home her mother had kept. She prepared the goose liver on Fridays. She arranged the table settings until they were perfect. Her cooking ensured that Apu's pace was brisk on his short mid-day walk home from work, since lunch was the main meal of the day in Europe. When he got home, the *húsleves* would be simmering in the pot, its bubbles sending small aromatic shocks into the air. The *krumpli* would be breathing puffs of steam at the ceiling. The *rántott hús* would be pounded and breaded, the cutlets placed in rows, the eggs beaten, the breadcrumbs arranged, and the meat fried until golden brown. Anyu gave Dad a tiny piece, extra crispy, before Apu got home. She'd later take the leftover grease used to fry the chicken and boil it with a cleaning agent, cooling the mixture and cutting it into bars. Those bars became the soap she used to wash their clothes.

Dinner that night would be something light — perhaps a sandwich or sardines. Before bed, Dad would walk up a flight of stairs to a neighbor's apartment. She was expecting his knock. It came every night, without exception. When she opened the door, he reached out his hand. A white sugar cube was dropped on his palm. He smiled and said thank you. With his treat already in his mouth, Dad would run downstairs with one purpose: to find his brother.

Lutzi was eight years older than Dad. He was built like Apu: big and muscular with olive skin and dark hair. Girls in town went out of their way to say hello to him, even smiling at the small boy who was always by his side. The girls would whisper when they saw the two of them riding around town on the bicycle they shared, the big brother peddling, the little brother on the handlebars. Lutzi was usually the first pick for soccer games by the river and was such a good dancer that an instructor asked Anyu why she'd brought him for lessons in the first place.

There are only a few surviving photos of Dad and his brother. In one of them, they are standing on a beach, both wearing Speedo-like swimsuits. Dad might have been seven; Lutzi was around 15. In the picture, my uncle's legs are long, his torso tight, his chest showing the sinews of a developing physique. His face curves naturally, and his eyes are like almonds.

When Jews got back from the concentration camps, families happened quickly, since creating life had never felt more important. The first child after the War held special significance. A doctor and a nurse came to the house for Lutzi's delivery. It was a Friday. Anyu didn't have drugs and didn't make a sound. Her neighbors knew she was going to give birth and were waiting for the screams to begin. They heard nothing. Anyu thought the energy she'd use to scream would be better served pushing. Her first baby weighed more than 4.5 kilograms, nearly 10 pounds. He arrived on June 13, 1947.

The name on his birth certificate said *Lutzi*. Anyu and Apu called him *Lutzike*. When they came to the United States, he went by his American name, Leslie. It's my middle name, in his honor. Dad called his brother *kiraikam*. In Hungarian, it means "my king."

chapter 9

mind & body

I WAS ONLY INTERESTED IN TWO THINGS AFTER MISSING the shot against Alabama in the NCAA Tournament: healing and hope. Instead of spending the summer at Stanford with my teammates, I lived with Anyu in her Bay Area apartment. Every day, I worked out in San Francisco with a man called "Hell's Trainer." His other nicknames included "The Mental Patient," "The Genetic Freak," and, appropriately, "Crazy Frank." I knew him simply as Frank.

Frank was originally from New Jersey but had moved to the Bay Area around the same time I got to Stanford. We'd been family friends for years, and he'd been trying to get me to work out with him since I arrived on campus. He'd tell me that what I did at school, with a top college basketball program, was what he called "illusion training."

My body had changed significantly over the years. The pale pile of skin and bones who'd dropped out of Hebrew school was gone. I was still extraordinarily pale, but now I was 6'6", 220 pounds, with 6 percent body fat. I'd remind Frank of that fact. "Irrelevant, sir," Frank would say. "You've never really worked out, sir. You're kidding yourself, sir. You wouldn't last 10 minutes with me, sir."

As an important point of clarification: Frank calls all men "sir."

Everywhere he went, Frank wore boots, basketball shorts, an army vest, sunglasses, and a fisherman's hat to cover his buzzed head. His Siberian Husky, Seminole, was always by his side. Frank is the only person I know who has landed in Las Vegas during the summer and run more than four miles on the side of the highway — from the airport to his hotel on the Strip — in the 110-degree heat, just to get a workout in. It's not completely possible for another human being to understand Frank, but the image of a man in combat boots, a tactical vest, and a black fisherman's hat running on the shoulder of a Las Vegas highway on a scorching summer day is as good of a starting point as one can expect.

Frank's training would eventually be featured on ESPN because it was so unorthodox and effective. He made sure his face was blacked out and his voice encrypted for the interview. The reason? Who the hell knows? That's just Frank. He used to train people for the military and has since treated everyone he's met like he's training them for the military.

The first time we worked out was a Saturday in the spring, about a month after I missed the shot against Alabama. Frank had been begging me to try his training just once to see what I could actually be doing with my body and mind. To put myself back together following the Alabama game, I knew I'd need to prepare differently. I knew I'd need to do more than anyone else. I knew it would need to hurt. The time was right to try some crazy shit, and Frank was some crazy shit.

I met him on the sand hills of a San Francisco beach at 8:00 AM to start the first part of our workout. "Good morning, sir," Frank said with a smile when I arrived. "It's another gorgeous day in San Francisco, isn't it, sir?"

I glanced around. It was foggy and windy and looked like it was about to rain.

"Shall we, sir?" Frank said, pointing to the sand hill he'd picked out for our workout. I stepped onto the sand. It was so thick that my feet sank in up to my ankles. First, Frank told me to walk up and down the hill to warm up. He walked right next to me. My quads and hamstrings burned trying to lift my body up the incline. After a few minutes, Frank told me to jog up and down the sand hill. There was nothing for my legs to push against. "Now sprint, please, sir," Frank finally said. He sprinted next to me. My chest started to tighten.

Soon, it was a mixture of walk, jog, sprint. "One walk up and down the hill, please, sir," he'd say. "One jog, please, sir. Two sprints, please, sir."

After 15 minutes, my temples began to throb. My vision blurred. Frank was breezing right past me on the hill, his breath steady. He was wearing an 84-pound weight vest. All the while, he was taunting me. "You can run to Grandma's at any time, sir." "Grandma will have the food on the table as soon as you want, sir." "Still think you've been training hard, sir?"

When Frank saw I was close to passing out, he waited one extra minute, just to see if I'd quit. When he was convinced I wouldn't, he pulled me off the hill, cutting that part of the workout in half. "Your mind will always give out before your body, sir," he said as I slumped into the car.

On the drive to our next location, I stared vacantly out the window. Any lifeforce I'd had in my body had been left on that sand hill. When I stepped out of the car for the next phase of the workout, I couldn't root myself to the Earth. I felt like I might tumble right off it. My legs wobbled until I had to grab the car for support. I saw a unicorn in the bushes chatting with a T-Rex, so that was memorable. When Frank looked into my googly hallucinating eyes, he called it a day. "That's enough, sir," he said. "You're done, and you did well. Let's get you to Grandma's."

Still in a daze, I called Anyu on my way home. The food was on the table when I walked in. On the phone later that night, Frank told me that one in seven elite athletes came back for more of his training. "Let's see how serious you are about being great, sir," he said.

It was just me and Frank — three days on, one day off — for three sessions a day, all summer long. Frank's training was as extreme as my need to prove myself. I'd never been afraid of work, but now, for the first time, I had a chance to find out how far I was willing to go. Crazy Frank and his crazy training were specifically engineered to test a person's limits. I didn't just endure Frank's training; I consumed it like a drug.

On a normal day, we were together from 9:00 AM until 7:00 PM. We worked in the sand a lot, but we also sprinted steps and did backward circuits up hills, a variety of push-ups and pull-ups, pause-squats, plyometric jumps, hanging holds, swims, wooders, dirty dogs, step-ups, and an exercise called "save the kids" that required me to shuffle along two parallel bars in pull-up position, using only my arms, from one side of a playground platform to the other. The exercise mimicked traversing a body of water to save stranded kids on the other side, hence the name.

We'd eat a huge lunch, then I'd take an afternoon nap in Frank's apartment to get ready for the night session, which usually involved basketball drills and more strength training. His apartment was a studio in San Francisco. The only furniture inside was a bed, a folding chair, and a plyo ball to sit on. In the small kitchen there was one plate, one fork, one spoon, and one knife. I covered myself in an old blanket and passed out on the bed next to Seminole. His white Husky hair was everywhere, but I didn't care. I could've slept anywhere.

With Frank, I'd end an hour-long run in the sand by sprinting the finish, and as soon as I'd cross the line, he'd tell me I had another 15-minute trip up and down the beach. Trying to catch my breath, I'd scream and curse and tell him to do things to himself that friends really shouldn't tell other friends to do to themselves. Most of the stuff I said wasn't even anatomically possible, but Frank wouldn't flinch. He'd just stand there with his arms crossed, his sunglasses and fisherman's hat straight as arrows. He'd pat Seminole's head. "Another lap, please, sir."

I'd give him the finger and do the lap.

As hard as Frank pushed me physically, the core of his training was mental. Like everyone, I'd constructed guardrails in my mind for what I was and wasn't capable of. Over the course of my life, my mind had learned to send signals to my body, warning me of my limitations. Frank taught me how to block those signals. He said that we all have a voice in our head that tells us what we can't, shouldn't, or won't do. Unlocking the power of the human will, he insisted, was as simple as being able to tell that voice to shut the fuck up. "Your mind will always give out before your body, sir," Frank kept repeating.

As I continued to work, the sand hills that dominated me early on became too easy. I eventually moved to steeper and thicker ones. After a few weeks, I could do 10-mile runs on the beach and twice as many pull-ups as when I started — even while wearing a 30-pound weight vest. My rapid progress wasn't surprising to Frank. He said I'd simply unleashed potential that had been there all along. Now that my mind was out of the way, my body could become what it was meant to become.

Every morning at 5:00 AM, I'd eat a mix of brown rice, olive oil, parmesan cheese, and grilled chicken breast, per Frank's orders. Anyu hated that I was eating this concoction for breakfast, but she made it for me every night. When I'd roll out of bed and stumble to the fridge, the meal would be waiting for me, the plastic wrap meticulously tucked under the edges of the dish, the chicken perfectly yet begrudgingly prepared.

During our daily basketball drills at the YMCA, I'd shoot a thousand three-pointers. Frank tallied my makes and misses. Some days, I'd be in the gym for hours, after having been on the sand for hours. At the time, I would've said that I was a man possessed. In reality,

97

it was fear that was driving me. I couldn't deal with feeling so inadequate. I had a relentless need to live up to my history. I was scared that I didn't have enough strength, so I worked on my strength so I'd no longer feel scared. On the last day of my summer with Frank, he put me through a five-hour circuit of cardio in the sand, training on the pull-up bar, and drills on the basketball court. "If I had to, I could do another five hours," I told Frank when I finished.

"Very good, sir," Frank said, extending his arm for a fist pound. "Very good."

When I got back to Stanford in the fall, my mind and body had hardened. I had to see a doctor because my fingers were swollen from shooting so many jump shots over the summer. I smiled as the doctor examined my hands and said I'd worked them more than they could handle. I felt a strange power that came from suffering for what I wanted.

My coach at Stanford, Mike Montgomery, had been hired to be the head coach of the Golden State Warriors after our historic year, so I had a fresh start at Stanford under Trent Johnson, a former Cardinal assistant who was hired away from the University of Nevada.

Before the season, we ran our yearly mile race as a team to see who was ready to compete. I won the mile with a time of 5:05 — 20 seconds faster than I'd run the year before. After a week of practice, my play had been relentless, unglamorous, and punishing, a slow and unsexy style in the mold of one of my basketball heroes, Larry Bird. I remember calling my dad. "You're not going to believe what's happening," I said.

It hadn't even been a year since I'd crippled myself mentally every time I stepped on the floor. I had our video coordinator send my dad a tape of one of our practices. I needed him to see for himself. Before our first game, I sat with Frank, Anyu, and my parents in the stands at Oracle Arena, home of the Warriors. I stared straight ahead, my gaze fixed. "Are you okay, honey?" my mom asked, sensing that my mood was unlike anything she'd seen from me.

"He's ready," Frank answered. "That's all."

We beat the University of San Francisco at Oracle that night. I had 23 points and 11 rebounds, both new career highs for me at Stanford. The next game, I had 19 points and eight rebounds against Tennessee, Dad's alma mater. Then 20 points and seven rebounds against BYU. Three games into the season, I was averaging 20.7 points and nine rebounds per game. An article came out in the newspaper naming me as an NBA prospect. Someone from Stanford's chapter of Hillel, the international organization dedicated to Jewish campus life, stopped me on campus and called me "Jewish Jordan."

Thanks to one crazy summer and three measly games, I was now the player I'd dreamt of becoming. I convinced myself that no one thought it was legitimate. Each time I played it was to prove it wasn't a fluke. As preparation, I'd write a short script before every game, a detailed visualization of what I wanted to happen from the time I entered the gym. It would always include a moment when I looked around the arena at all the people who'd once laughed at me. I'd work myself into a frenzy, allowing the voice in my head to say: *no one believes in you, no one respects you, no one notices you.*

By the middle of my junior season at Stanford, still less than a year after missing the shot against Alabama, after struggling not to humiliate myself on the court, after being the worst player on my team, I was the second-leading scorer in the Pac-10 Conference. I was a top-10 three-point-shooter and a top-20 rebounder in the conference. I went from 23 percent from three to 43. I went from averaging 3.4 points per game to 18, the highest increase in the country and in the history of Stanford's basketball program. I had 29 points in a home win against Arizona. I had 25 points and eight rebounds in Pauley Pavilion to beat UCLA. Another 26 against Santa Clara and 24 against Arizona State. And on and on. Not only was I producing, but we were also winning games. I relished every opportunity to fight alongside my teammates, guys who'd become like brothers to me.

USA Basketball asked me to join the national team, like my dad once had, and I was projected as a potential first-round pick in the NBA Draft, like my dad had once been. There were 20 guys in the conference that year who'd go on to play in the NBA. They'd make more than $350 million combined. I had become one of the top players in that group. The best part was that my ascension was built on perseverance, a defining family value that I'd never felt truly belonged to me.

I made a point not to talk about my success. I just kept my head down and played. I was scared that by talking about what was happening, it would somehow disappear. The tic in my eye that had given me such problems over the years was gone now, like it was something from another life. ESPN was complimenting my game, like I'd told them they'd be. I had agents trying to get in touch with me and opposing coaches talking about me with admiration. After a game against Louisville, their legendary coach, Rick Pitino, pulled me close while we were shaking hands and said in my ear, "Danny, I've never in my life seen a son who plays as much like his father as you play like your dad."

I'd reached the top of a mountain, known only to me, sacred only to me. I'd become an absolute animal on the basketball court. I now know that the peak of my climb was right before a fast break against Cal at home on February 12, 2005. It was a few days after my 21st birthday. I was hearing rumblings by then that I should leave Stanford after the season to enter the NBA Draft early, since my stock had risen so much. I had a chance to join my dad as one of the highest Jewish draft picks of all time.

The game against Cal was on national television. Tiger Woods, a Stanford alum and one of the most famous people on the planet, was sitting courtside. Anyu was in her usual seat behind our second-half basket, her white hair sprayed to a glossy shine, her posture straight, her smile proud.

They say you never know you're in your glory days until you leave them. I wish I would've known that this moment would be the pinnacle of my basketball career. I already had 16 points, and it was still early in the second half. I was locked in and cooking, having settled into a sweet rhythm. My team had just gotten a steal, which meant that if I could outrun everyone, like I'd been doing all season, I'd get another bucket, bringing my tally to 18. Grit had become my identity. My dad told me after one game that my toughness was overwhelming my opponents. I got goose bumps from hearing that, which shows how badly I needed to hear that.

Seeing two more points in my future, I put my head down and ran toward Anyu. My eyes narrowed. My jaw clenched. I furiously pumped my arms and legs. My feet slammed onto the hardwood to propel me forward. I'd sprinted the sand hills with Frank so many times that summer. This felt routine. I was ruthlessly prepared, and I'd do anything to get this layup. With each step, I moved closer to Anyu, who was sitting behind the basket.

I outran the competition and angled toward the hoop. I'd earned an easy bucket. My point guard delivered the pass as I barreled toward the basket. I planted my outside leg to make the catch and elevate to the rim to finish the play. When my foot made contact with the court, stabilizing my body and creating enough force to lift me upward, a bolt of energy shot through my right leg. I knew right away what had happened.

Without warning and without apology, my knee ripped apart.

The ball flew out of my hands as I collapsed to the floor. I grabbed my knee and started screaming. With my forehead pressed to the court, my body writhing beneath me, I pounded my fist on the ground and yelled "why?" It's the only question to ask when a dream is destroyed. It took me a minute to regain my focus, and when I did, our team trainer was kneeling beside me. His hand was on my back to calm me down. He whispered in my ear, "Did you hear a pop?"

His voice was composed, but I was hysterical. "I think so," I heaved between breaths.

In reality, I knew so. I got hurt on the baseline, 20 feet from where Anyu always sat. When I finally came to my senses, I realized she was on the floor next to me, rubbing my head. I still have no idea how she got down there so fast.

chapter 10

smugglers & icon

B EFORE THE HOLOCAUST, MY GRANDFATHER WAS asked to represent Romania in an international Ping-Pong tournament held in Romania's capital city of Bucharest. Apu was barely 20 years old but already a top Ping-Pong player in the country. He was a defender, a pusher, someone who prowled with his paddle and never took a risk. He simply waited for his opponent to make a mistake.

He was driven to compete against the best, but participating in the prestigious tournament in Bucharest came with a stipulation: Romanian officials insisted he use the last name Campeanu instead of Grunfeld. The Romanian authorities were concerned that Grunfeld sounded too Jewish. They wanted to distance themselves from anything having to do with the Jews, so they settled on Campeanu, a secular Romanian name. Apu refused to compete in the event. His thinking on the subject was pretty straightforward: no fucking way.

At 6'3" with a narrow waist and broad shoulders, Apu had thick hair and dark skin. His mustache was prominent and his cheekbones sharp. His countenance straddled the line between dignified and dangerous. He could've passed for a police chief, a mafia boss, or both. Ping-Pong was his best sport, but in the years leading up to the Holocaust, he starred at goalie for Sanitas, a Jewish soccer team in Satu Mare, Romania. When the team of Romanian Jews ran out to take the field, Apu led the way. His generous calves fired as his cleats dug into the grass. There'd be a soccer ball spinning on his finger. Apu was working a job selling tools in a hardware store when he was sent to a labor camp in Hungary. I remember asking Anyu why he didn't run when he was summoned. "Run where?" was her response.

All things considered, Apu's life in the camp could have been much worse. His most traumatic moment occurred as he was driving a mule-drawn cart filled with supplies down an abandoned road. That's when his camp took fire from planes that had appeared overhead. Bullets sliced through the air, and Apu jumped out of the cart, diving into a roadside ditch to seek cover from the spray of machine guns. A bomb pounded the road he'd been traveling on. As flames and debris rained, Apu huddled in his ditch. Suddenly, he was jolted forward with a thud as something slammed into his back. He was knocked flat onto his stomach, unable to right himself. After the attack planes passed, he made his way out of the ditch and discovered what had crashed into him. It was the top half of one of the mules. A bomb had blown the animal apart at the belly.

Apu was in the camp in Hungary with Joe, his best friend from Transylvania. They both worked as cooks in the camp. Neither of them had ever prepared a real meal, but they could dump scraps into a boiling pot. There wasn't much food to go around, but as cooks, they at least got more than the others. The Nazi guards found out that Apu was a good soccer player and sometimes let him kick the ball around with them. Even Nazis liked soccer.

Apu was liberated in August of 1944. Both of his parents and his one stepparent had been killed in Auschwitz. His two sisters had died on a Nazi death march. One collapsed on the side of the road, her head swollen, and refused to go on. The other sat on one of the carts placed by the Nazis for those who'd given up. A friend begged her to continue, to no avail. She stayed seated on the cart, which took her to her death.

After returning from the War, all Apu had was time and work. He cobbled money together and opened a shoe store in Satu Mare.

The day after Anyu got back from the Budapest Ghetto, she walked through his doors. Her blonde hair shined, but her face was slim and severe. Apu was used to seeing that look in those who'd survived. Anyu visited the store with her brother, Bala, a friend of Apu's who'd been in the same labor camp in Hungary.

They'd come in search of new clothes, since Anyu only had three items of clothing to her name: her worn cotton dress, her inherited pair of men's pants, and the navy blue jacket that was her only protection from the cold in the ghetto. Frayed and filthy, the clothes were all in shambles, barely wearable. Entering Apu's store, Anyu had on her sister Shari's overcoat, which was in much better shape than her own. Shari was a heavy woman, and since Anyu was naturally thin, made thinner by the War, her sister's big and boxy coat enveloped her. The coat puffed outward at the stomach and the back. "Bala's sister is very pretty," Apu said when she left his store, "but she's the size of a cow."

He was right on one account.

Anyu and Apu were married at her parents' house in Micula less than a year later, in a double ceremony with Anyu's sister, Bubby, the only family member who returned from Auschwitz. The wedding was held in November of 1945, nine months after the death camp was liberated. To celebrate the wedding in Micula, Anyu and her two sisters cooked at home for 30 or so guests. The Holocaust had complicated Jewish observance, so the only religious element of the ceremony was the construction of a small chuppah, the canopy under which Jews are wed. The ovens in the death camps incinerated customs, too, but the chuppah was proof that an ember of Jewishness still burned.

Anyu and her sister had no father to give them away or mother to give them advice, yet Anyu smiled as she ate her *libamáj*. She no longer believed in God, but she'd always believe in family. As her father had told her, family was the most important thing to a Jew. This was her opportunity to build one. While her guests followed their *rántott hús* with warm servings of *almas pite*, Anyu coughed quietly into her napkin. She had pneumonia on her wedding day, but she didn't mention it to anyone. It was nothing to complain about.

At the time of the wedding, as Anyu's life was being rebuilt, a new professional basketball league was starting across the ocean. In November of the following year, the New York Knicks would play the Toronto Huskies in the inaugural game of the Basketball Association of America, the league that would become the NBA. The Knicks' starting lineup for the first NBA game — Ralph Kaplowitz, Ossie Schectman, Sonny Herzberg, Jake Weber, and Leo Gottlieb — was 100 percent Jewish. These men were American and thus had avoided the Holocaust. Ossie Schectman from Kew Gardens, Queens, scored the NBA's first basket. The Jews on the Knicks managed to lead them to victory over the Huskies 68-66. Throughout the NBA's inaugural season, anti-Semitic taunts against the Knicks rang louder and louder at Madison Square Garden. By the end of the next year, the Knicks had gotten rid of every Jewish player on the roster.

In the years following Anyu's wedding in Micula, a fog descended upon Romania. Communism had taken root following the Soviet occupation after World War II. Social classes, private property, and a profit-based economy were shunned in favor of common ownership, government control, and outright censorship. With all work nationalized, Apu lost his shoe store. The state gave him a job selling fruits and vegetables wholesale and then the job selling damaged and distressed goods. Every day, honest Romanians in Satu Mare were jailed and beaten for speaking a word against the government. The Holocaust was over in Europe, but sour winds still blew across the continent.

What the state paid its citizens for a month of labor could only buy food for a week. Stores rarely had meat. Anyu had a friend working in a slaughterhouse who'd slip meat in his pocket before leaving his post. Anyu would buy that black-market meat when the stores were empty. To set the menu for my uncle's Bar Mitzvah, Apu went into the countryside and bought a cow. The butcher handled the rest. The only way to get by in Communist Romania was to make extra money on the side. It was illegal but not shameful. It was a matter of survival. If an item cost 100 lei, Apu would charge 110 and pocket the spread. If someone requested two meters of fabric, he'd short it a bit and sell the difference for himself.

In an attempt to guard against impropriety, the communists searched homes for contraband and made threats with no evidence. They threw people in prison and tortured them for information. Anyu's friends burned their illegal money out of fear it would be discovered.

Anyu and Apu, though, exchanged their extra Romanian lei on the black market for American dollars. Their dealer brought dollars right to their house, always wearing his black frock coat and furry black top hat. His beard and side locks made him appear an unlikely mastermind for a money-laundering scheme. He was a Hasidic Jew.

It was still dangerous to be a Jew — regardless of occupation. People told jokes about Jews, excluded Jews, spit on Jews. The Hasidic money dealer was once questioned by the police and beaten until his skin looked like velvet, but he never said a word about his operation or his customers. Under the Iron Curtain, American dollars were far more dangerous than extra Romanian lei. Being caught with dollars led to jail and worse, but lei were weak compared to dollars, so it was worth the risk. Anyu and Apu hid their dollars at home in an old radio. During a search of the house, a communist officer once picked up the radio and demanded to see its registration. He threw it to the ground when the documentation could not be produced. He never bothered to look inside the radio. It stored thousands of dollars by then.

Apu continued to play Ping-Pong after the War, competing in the World Championships in Bucharest in 1953. He finished the competition as a top-100 ranked player in the world. He honed his skills by practicing with Angelica Rozeanu, the Romanian champion known as the greatest female player of all time. She and Apu were an even match. She's the only female player to win six straight world titles, but from 1940 to 1944, she wasn't allowed to enter a gymnasium in Romania to play Ping-Pong. Her given surname was Adelstein. She was Jewish.

When they left Romania, Apu and Anyu couldn't bring many possessions out, but Apu took his Ping-Pong paddles. My dad still has them. The handles are worn from decades of squeezing and gripping. The faces are faded from countless feathery contacts. Dad keeps the paddles in his closet next to his gold medal. They're a distant athletic legacy that lives on. Once in a while, we'll look at the paddles together.

My family spent a decade trying to find a way to leave Romania. They finally had an opportunity when, in 1963, Israel agreed to pay Romania $3,000 for each Jew it would allow to emigrate. Apu and Anyu's plan was to flee Communist Romania and head to the Jewish homeland as Israeli citizens. Anyu and Lutzi started taking Hebrew lessons. Dad was still young enough to learn the language once they got to Israel. Apu had no such benefit, but he figured he'd pick up Hebrew on the fly.

The Israeli passports soon arrived at the police station, meaning their Romanian citizenship would have to be renounced. Leaving their motherland made them traitors. They were instantly considered enemies of the state. They wouldn't be welcome to return and were prohibited from taking anything of value out of the country. Between the four of them, they were allowed two 70-kilogram crates along with a few small personal bags. Pants, socks, jackets, underwear, bedding, pillows, pots, and pans were stowed away while jewelry and fine materials had to be left behind. Taking out money was absolutely forbidden.

At the train station on the day of the departure, the communist officers patted down each family member before they boarded the train for Belgrade en route to Rome. Even my eight-year-old dad was ordered to keep his hands in the air as the police frisked him. Their luggage was thoroughly searched. The Ping-Pong paddles wrapped in underwear didn't rouse suspicion.

A communist officer eventually approached Anyu and demanded to know if they were carrying out money. She shook her head. She had nothing of value with her, she told them. Even her Rosenthal Porcelain had been left behind. Her voice still sparkles when describing the beige dishes with their circular maroon trim. "We even had a serving plate for fish," she says with pride. Anyu and Apu went back to Romania decades later and tried to track down the porcelain. They wanted to bring it to America. It was long gone by then.

The Romanian officer who'd questioned Anyu about the money had no way of knowing he'd already been deceived. In fairness, Anyu was telling the truth by saying that she wasn't carrying any money. What she neglected to share was that she didn't need to carry any money. My grandparents had already arranged to leave the country with all the Romanian lei and American dollars they had to their name.

They strategized for weeks on how to smuggle out the Romanian lei, which amounted to roughly $1,000. My grandparents knew everything would be searched extensively when boarding the train for Belgrade, so Apu hatched an idea. As they prepared to leave the country, they put all their black market lei inside the radio where they kept their dollars. The radio spoke the news, but it never told their secret.

Apu knew their train would stop in Serbia before heading to Rome, and that was all he needed to get started. He canvassed the streets for more information, tapping into his deep network of contacts and asking the right people the right questions until he found out the exact train carriage that would transport the family out of Romania. The night before their departure, Apu slipped out of the house under starless black skies. A friend accompanied as a lookout. They walked to the train station without saying a word. The train was parked in preparation for the trip to Rome the following day. Apu located the right carriage and forced his way on board. The wad of Romanian lei was buried deep in his pocket. He found a nondescript seat near the front of the train and stuck the cash underneath it, out of sight of anyone who might occupy the seat. He hurried off the train and carefully made his way home. His watchman assured him that no one had seen a thing.

When the train pulled away from Satu Mare the following day, Apu was already laughing with his boys and chatting with strangers on board. The journey was easy, and the stopover in Belgrade passed without issue. When the train reached the station in Rome, passengers began to disembark, but Apu moved slowly, hanging behind the fray. Once the crowd had cleared, he returned to the seat he'd visited the night before. The money was exactly where he'd left it.

With a grin on his face, he stuffed it in his pocket and stepped onto Italian soil. He had $1,000 worth of Romanian lei on him that the communists would never know about.

The American dollars were too risky to hide under a seat, but they got those out, too. They had accumulated nearly $4,000 over a long decade of scraping profits from nothing. It was a small fortune in those days. To take that much illegal money out of a communist bloc country was a case study in risk. They would've been jailed, tortured, or killed in Romania for possessing that many dollars. As Anyu and Apu searched for smuggling opportunities, their efforts were ironically and unexpectedly set in motion by a Hollywood feature film about smuggling. *The Golden Head* was being shot in Budapest at the time. It tells the story of a British family visiting the city for an international crime convention. The plot coalesces around the Stevenson boys, who trail thieves attempting to smuggle the golden bust of Saint Laszlo out of Hungary.

Anyu's first cousin from Budapest, György, was a young staffer on the movie set. Specifically, he served as the translator and personal assistant to the movie's biggest star, Buddy Hackett, a Jew from Brooklyn and one of America's most celebrated comedians. He made 87 appearances on *The Tonight Show* with Johnny Carson. Before his career in comedy, Buddy Hackett had served in the U.S. Army during World War II in an anti-aircraft battery. He took a liking to Anyu's cousin, a brainy Hungarian Jew who'd survived that war.

The plan Anyu and Apu came up with a few months before leaving Romania seemed crazy, but nothing could be considered crazy anymore. Anyu had a family member who'd seen starving Jews in Auschwitz chewing on the bones of the deceased for sustenance. The War had changed everything. Reason and rationality no longer applied.

My grandparents were trying to exploit a unique loophole: as an American celebrity, Buddy Hackett was allowed to carry around as many dollars as he pleased. He could cross international borders at any time without being questioned. If Anyu's cousin, György, could convince Buddy Hackett to carry the money back to America to then be sent to the family in Israel, the plan might work.

Getting the money from Satu Mare to Budapest would be dangerous, but it was doable. The hard part would be securing Buddy Hackett's participation. He was a global icon with nothing to gain from joining Holocaust survivors in a plot to smuggle illegal money out of a communist regime. When György nervously presented the idea to Buddy Hackett, the comedy legend didn't hesitate. "Bring me the money," he said. "I'll take care of the rest."

Anyu and Apu stared blankly at each other when they heard the news. Buddy Hackett would take their dollars to the States — no questions asked — and send them to Anyu's brother, Andy, who'd already settled in the Bronx. Anyu admired American celebrities like Clark Gable, Harry Belafonte, and Buddy Hackett, but their worlds couldn't have felt further apart. The universe was showing Anyu that worlds had a funny habit of colliding.

It was Anyu's responsibility to ensure the money's safe transport to Budapest. She'd always been good with her hands, and it was time for the performance of her life. She retrieved her sewing kit and laid out her supplies across the kitchen table. The blinds were drawn, but Anyu's back was still to the window. She grabbed a suitcase from the closet, carefully removed the lining, and created a false bottom in the case. She packed the money tight in the hidden compartment she'd made and then sewed the lining back over it. She compared her stitchwork to the original threading. The compartment was undetectable. The suitcase was ounces heavier, thousands of dollars more valuable, and now something that could result in many hard years of prison. To the naked eye, it looked exactly as it had before.

György's dad was Anyu's uncle — her late mother's brother who'd survived a concentration camp and five years as a Russian prisoner of war — and he volunteered to take the money to Budapest. When he arrived in Satu Mare to collect the suitcase for transfer, he couldn't figure out where the money was hidden. No one ever told him. Just don't draw attention to yourself, they said, and everything will be fine.

Anyu's uncle took the train to Budapest, suitcase in hand, and made the drop to György, who then delivered the goods to Buddy Hackett. Holding the case for the first time, Buddy Hackett crinkled his dumpling nose and peered over his horned-rimmed glasses. He couldn't figure out where the money was either. It wasn't until György cut open the compartment that the money touched Buddy Hackett's hands. The moment it did, it was no longer illegal. It now belonged to an American celebrity. It could pass freely into the United States, where it could one day be reunited with its original owners. All Buddy Hackett had to do was keep his word.

Twenty years later, Anyu wore a sequin dress and pearl earrings as she sat in a packed theater in Las Vegas watching Buddy Hackett perform. While vacationing with friends, my grandparents had bought tickets to see one of America's great comedy headliners. Anyu found Buddy Hackett's jokes crude, but she liked his closing bit when he talked about his son's Bar Mitzvah.

Over drinks after the show, Anyu told her friends about the good deed Buddy Hackett had done for them. She and Apu had never even met Buddy Hackett, Anyu said, but he'd taken out their money because they needed the help. Anyu had tears in her eyes during her retelling. A friend shook his head and excused himself from the table. He went to the front desk of the hotel. It took him the better part of an hour, but he was able to talk his way into Buddy Hackett's suite. He had an important message for the comedian, he said. Those immigrants from Romania, the ones with the suitcase and the dollars and the chutzpah, were at his show. And their little boy had even become a famous athlete in America — in New York City, nonetheless. "Bring them up!" Buddy Hackett yelled. Anyu's friend warned that it was a big group. "Bring them all up!"

Anyu and Apu talked the night away with Buddy Hackett in his suite, as equals, a thousand miles from where they'd started. As Buddy Hackett poured them fine liquor and reminisced about his time in Budapest, my grandma thanked him for taking their money to America and sending it to her brother's house in the Bronx. It was the money they had used to start their new life in the United States, she told him. She was especially grateful for the extra $50 Buddy Hackett had added from his own pocket, the equivalent of more than $1,000 today. "You didn't have to do that," Anyu told him.

"I know," he replied with a smile.

The comedian also smiled when Anyu reminded him of the note he'd written by hand and included with the money, which had his extra $50 sitting on top. She'd never forget his words. Neither will I. "Good luck in America," the note read. "Sincerely, Buddy Hackett."

chapter 11

pain & progress

A NYU STAGGERED BACK TO HER SEAT AFTER MY INJURY. Assisted by team trainers, I hopped off the court on one leg. Murmurs in the arena began to cut the silence. Frank leaned over the railing. "Dude, is it your ankle?" he yelled down to me. He didn't call me "sir." That should've been the first indication that something was wrong.

"Call my mom and tell her I'm okay," is all I said back.

The game against Cal was on national television, so I knew my mom, dad, and sister were watching. If anyone was feeling my pain at that moment, it was my mom. My trainers led me through the curtains that separated the court from the back hallway. As soon as we disappeared from sight, I asked them to stop. They held me upright. It was just the three of us now. My arms rested on their shoulders, and my right leg dangled above the floor. I brought my hands to my face and started crying. I'd been so close. My trainers let me cry for as long as I needed. They propped me up and supported me until I caught my breath and signaled to keep moving.

With my pulse raging, my chest rising and falling, a team doctor checked the stability of my knee in the training room. He shifted it side to side and back and forth, examining it for structural damage. I studied his face for hints, but his countenance stayed steady. He said we'd need to get an MRI to understand more. The doctor left the training room to arrange the test. From the court, I heard our fans cheer for a made basket. The world had moved on without me, as it should have, since the world waits for no one. I'd gone from being the second-leading scorer in the conference and an NBA draft pick to being damaged goods, unable to walk. It had only taken a second.

I didn't know much about knee injuries up to that point. The most exposure I'd had to them was talking about Bernard King's famous injury when I was a kid. He and my dad were playing for the Knicks at the time. Uncle B was leading the NBA in scoring at 32.9 points per game when he went down. Dad will always remind people that Bernard became an All-Star again, even after missing two full years for his recovery. No one had ever done that before, Dad says with pride.

As I was lying on the table trying to calm down, with my hands folded on my chest and my eyes closed, I heard footsteps approaching. The door opened. "Tatele," Anyu said.

A team official escorted her into the training room. She'd been to every game I played at Stanford, but she'd never been in the back before. A silver slope of Anyu's hair was hanging to the side. Even her Aqua Net couldn't withstand the stress of the moment. She sat on a stool by the training table and grabbed my hand. The doctors left us alone. "Tatele, are you okay?" she asked, her voice shaking.

"I worked hard, Anyu," is all I could say.

I started to cry again.

Basketball had always presided over my life in a complicated way. With one step, it had all become more complicated. I wondered if my dad would've cried if this had happened to him. *No way*, I thought.

An MRI taken at the hospital after the game confirmed that I'd torn my ACL, like Bernard King had 20 years prior. I had dinner that night at the Cheesecake Factory with Anyu and Frank. The Crusted Chicken Romano had no chance of easing the pain of my torn knee ligament. Even the comfort of *rántott hús* and *meggyleves* wouldn't have lasted long.

No fans were asking for my autograph now. No media members were praising my game. No agents were looking for me. My leg was cinched in a thigh-high brace, and my crutches were lean-ing against the wall. My phone buzzed with messages from family and friends as news of my injury hit the ticker on ESPN. My dad had already called three times. He said he'd come out to California for my surgery, which was set for 10 days later to give time for the swelling to subside.

Over dinner that night, Anyu, Frank, and I reflected on my season. From 3.4 points per game to 18. From a punchline to a first-team All-Conference selection. I'd go on to win numerous awards for my performance including, much to Anyu's satisfaction, the Marty Glickman Outstanding Jewish Scholastic Athlete of the Year. The ceremony was held at the Jewish Sports Hall of Fame in Commack, New York, where my dad was an inductee. I'd miss it while rehab-bing my knee.

Usually, when I ate with Frank, he didn't let me have dessert. It's not something I was allowed to consider. That night, he ordered me two pieces of Oreo cheesecake and made sure I finished them. "You deserve it, sir," Frank said.

Anyu told me she was proud of me. So did Frank.

"By the way, sir," Frank started as my second Oreo cheesecake plate was being cleared, "we have a lot of work to do. Next season's mile race is about eight months from tonight. You won it this year and you're going to win it again next year."

I rolled my eyes. "Whatever, Frank," I said.

"Sir, I'm serious," he said. "Don't let your mind tell your body you can't do it. You're going to win that race. You with me?"

I looked at my knee brace. It would be months before I could jog — let alone run, let alone sprint. I'd told Frank he was a lunatic a thousand times before, but on this one, I just didn't have the energy. "Okay, I'll win it again," I said.

Anyu let me sleep in her bed after my surgery. She slept on the couch in the living room. Dad slept on the pullout in the guest room. Anyu's guest room was where I stayed every summer. It was like my second bedroom. On the guest room wall, there was a proclamation announcing "Ernie Grunfeld Day" in the State of Tennessee. There were multiple All-American awards from his time in college. There were cartoon drawings of Dad's face from various newspapers across the country, needlepoint action shots made by fans, a set of Ernie Grunfeld fishing poles, Olympic credentials from Montreal, a framed *Sports Illustrated* cover with his face on it, tournament championship trophies, tournament MVP trophies, an SEC Player of the Year trophy. "Everyone has a scrap book," he'd say.

"Not as thick as yours," I'd counter.

The anterior cruciate ligament, the one I injured, is the major ligament in the knee that connects the thighbone to the shinbone. It's the ligament most responsible for providing stability to the knee joint. My ACL tore all the way through. There was also damage to my meniscus, the cartilage that provides cushioning for the joint. During the procedure at Stanford Hospital, my surgeon replaced my ruptured ACL with a section of my patellar tendon. He did it by breaking off pieces of bone on both sides of the patella, removing a portion of the tendon, and surgically implanting it where the ACL had been.

For a week after surgery, I peed in a clear plastic bottle beside the bed. Anyu would empty the contents for me several times a day. It was a callback to her time carrying Dad's baby poop to the outhouse in Romania. I didn't drink or do drugs, so I had no tolerance for the Percocet and Vicodin I was taking. I was numb for days, unable to feel the pain or feel my face. The most troubling part of my recovery was that I barely had an appetite to eat the food Anyu brought me. For me to refuse anything she cooked was absolute sacrilege. It was unthinkable, a real *shanda* for all parties involved. It's not a phase either one of us likes to talk about.

It was nearly spring break, so I could at least heal without worrying about missing class. During the school year, I skipped weekend pool parties to edit papers and packed notebooks in my gym bag so I could study on the bus during road trips. I approached school with my grandparents' immigrant mentality. I couldn't have explained what I was trying to prove. I only knew I had something to prove.

My work in the classroom at Stanford ultimately paid off. I was nominated for a Rhodes Scholarship by a professor of mine and was starting the application process when I got hurt. I wanted to play in the NBA after college, not study abroad in England, so I knew I wouldn't accept the scholarship even if I were selected. I guess I wanted to try to win the scholarship to show people that I could. It's a testament to my deep need to be seen. I wish I could've turned down the nomination, satisfied and comfortable with myself and my abilities, but that wasn't where I was. I needed others to know my worth. I didn't have quite enough of it on my own. The injury put an end to it all, anyway. I had to withdraw from the process to focus on my rehab.

It took me a week to be able to get out of bed and move around on crutches after surgery. I couldn't shower, so Anyu used a sponge to clean my back and shoulders. "That time I got a sponge bath from grandma" is not usually what guys brag about while recounting college glory days. Still, the warmth was soothing, and my body odor was kept in check. I regret nothing.

At my first appointment one-week post-surgery, the doctor changed my bandages, and I saw my new knee for the first time. It looked like a slab of roast beef. It was barely a knee at all, just a mound of puffy red flesh. Winning our team mile on that thing in less than eight months would be impossible, but I didn't tell Frank that.

The first challenge after surgery was being able to bend my knee again. I spent six hours a day lying on Anyu's living room floor with my right leg in a range-of-motion machine that bent and straightened my knee at a preset angle. I started around 15 or 20 degrees, hardly any movement at all. When the knee bent, the swelling pooled, and my traumatized joint screamed in protest. Each day, I increased the angle and dealt with the pain. Anyu would make sure I had pillows for my neck and back. She'd bring me snacks, and though my appetite was still limited, I did my best. Since I knew I'd be spending the majority of my day on the floor, I committed to using the time wisely. I set a goal to read several of the classic novels I'd never gotten to. *Of Mice and Men, War and Peace*, and *Anna Karenina* headlined the list. My plan was to come out of rehab culturally and intellectually enriched.

I never picked up any of those books and watched five seasons of the hit TV show *24* instead. I had no bandwidth for books — only Kiefer Sutherland killing bad guys all day long. I spent roughly 100 hours in the weeks after surgery on Anyu's floor with my leg in the range-of-motion machine, watching the show. I still haven't touched any of those books, but I've seen every season of *24*.

I quickly discovered that ACL recovery meant relearning how to fire my quad, which had become so atrophied that I could no longer flex it. When I tried to activate the muscle, it just lay there like melted butter. It meant schlepping myself around campus on crutches for a month, much to the chagrin of my surprisingly delicate armpits, which after a few days began to chafe. It meant learning to walk again, with an emphasis on striking my heel to the ground before the sole of my foot to apply appropriate pressure through the leg. I practiced at night by limping laps around Anyu's apartment

A portrait of Anyu's parents, one of only a few surviving photos of the pair.

Anyu, her parents, and her three younger siblings attend the wedding of her oldest sister, Shari, prior to World War II.

Anyu in her twenties, a few years after surviving the War.

My dad and his older brother in their winter attire in Romania, before the family left for Italy and eventually the United States.

My grandfather, Apu, with my uncle, Lutzi, as a baby in Romania.

Anyu poses with her young sons next to a European motorcycle during my dad's early years in Romania.

Apu (second from left) stands with his Ping-Pong teammates. Apu was a world-ranked player and standout athlete.

My dad and Anyu prior to leaving Romania.

A special portrait of my dad and his brother.

Far left: My uncle wears his high school cap and gown, shortly before his death.

Left: My dad as an adolescent, alone in New York after his brother passed away.

My dad plays for Forest Hills High School in Queens against crosstown rival DeWitt Clinton High School from the Bronx.

During his senior year at the University of Tennessee, my dad attacks the basket against Kentucky's Jack Givens. (AP Images)

My dad and Bernard King earned acclaim and the nickname the "Ernie and Bernie Show" while combining for nearly 50 points per game at Tennessee.

Anyu and my dad pose in front of his many high school and college trophies and plaques, a collection that would eventually cover an entire room in Anyu's apartment.

My dad shoots over Jim McMillian during his sophomore NBA season with the Milwaukee Bucks. (Getty Images)

While with the Kansas City Kings, the second of his three NBA stops, my dad fights for position with his friend, Paul Westphal. (Getty Images)

Back home in New York City, my dad wears the symbolic No. 18 for the New York Knicks during the last leg of his NBA career. (AP Images)

My dad and I enjoy basketball together after Knicks practice.

I started my days reading about the New York Knicks in the morning paper.

I'm in a Knicks T-shirt (as usual) with my sister, Becky, and my mom, Nancy.

My sister and I with our dad at a 1993 press conference announcing his promotion to vice president and general manager of the Knicks. (AP Images)

Driving to the hoop against Cal during the 2004-05 season. After struggling as an underclassman at Stanford, I found my groove and became one of the top scorers in the conference. (AP Images)

Our team trainers help me off the court after I tore my ACL, a career-altering injury that occurred when I was playing the best basketball of my life. (AP Images)

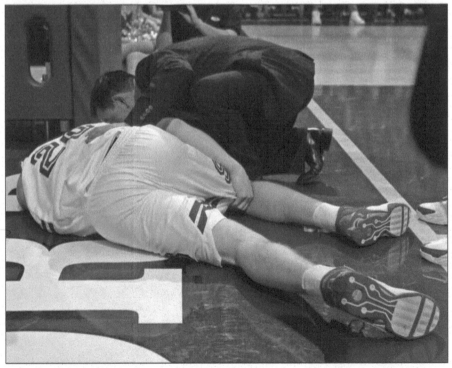

I immediately knew that something serious had happened to my knee. The ACL injury, right in the midst of my breakout season, was devastating. (AP Images)

My professional basketball career took me all over the world, from Germany to Spain to Israel and many places in between. I also achieved a childhood dream of playing for the New York Knicks, the team I grew up loving, in 2008. (AP Images)

Anyu makes magic in the kitchen as she cooks some of her incredible Hungarian food for her family.

My wife, Sam, and I spend time with Anyu. After considerable practice, Sam has learned to cook many of Anyu's dishes.

An American family with a European past: my mom, my sister, my dad, and me.

while she watched *Wheel of Fortune* or old Chabad telethons. When I'd make it to her bedroom, I'd see Pat Sajak and Vanna White or dancing rabbis and Hasidic magicians.

Recovery meant icing my knee several times during the day and every night before I went to bed. It meant gaining back the 20 pounds of muscle I'd lost. It meant hours on the underwater treadmill, hours on the stationary bike, and hours doing backward walks at an incline. It meant four days a week of squats, step-ups, box jumps, balance work, hamstring curls, cone drills, calf raises, and every other leg strengthening exercise in the book.

After four months, I could jog again. After a few weeks more, I could run. Then I could sprint and cut. Finally, after more than five months, I could shoot jump shots and do light drills on the basketball court. All the while, the mile race lingered in the back of my mind. I'd run a mile for the first time at four-and-a-half-months post-op. It took me eight minutes. I was about three minutes off from a time that could win, but the race became my North Star. I started mentioning it to Frank instead of the other way around.

To end the summer, I spent a month on the sand hills with Frank. He wore the same boots, shorts, vest, sunglasses, fisherman's hat, and had the same Siberian Husky, Seminole, by his side. It took some time to get reacquainted with his special brand of torture. I was six-months post-op by then. I hadn't been home all summer and only joined my family for a small portion of our summer vacation. It was all rehab, all the time. I wore a black knee brace for everything Frank and I did. Near the end of the summer, my dad visited and watched me work out for a few days. I showed him that I could dunk the basketball again. I hadn't been timed on the mile since my eight-minute clip when I first started running, but I knew I'd gotten stronger since then.

One afternoon when my dad was in town, toward the end of my time with Frank, I ran a timed practice mile. It was two weeks before the actual race was set to take place. My durability and stamina had been improving, but I needed to see if my North Star was actually reachable. I warmed up for a few minutes, made sure my knee brace was snug and secure, and then took my place at the starting line. I was all alone on the track. The sun was beating down on my neck. My stomach was rumbling. I was scared I wouldn't be close. Frank stood outside the fence with a timer in his hand, like the NBA's best coach, Red Auerbach, had done decades prior while watching Dad run a mile race at the Olympic trials. Dad was next to Frank. He was now the one doing the evaluating. I had beads of sweat on my forehead before Frank yelled "go."

From the very start, my legs felt tight. After the first lap, my chest was boiling. I thought about quitting. I couldn't believe it crossed my mind, especially with my dad watching, but it did. I felt like I might collapse. Stopping the run was the only way to end the distress. "Your mind will always give out before your body, sir," Frank would say.

For whatever reason — probably because my dad was there — I didn't stop running. I just kept my head down and accepted the pain. On my last lap, I tried to push, though I didn't have much left. When I crossed the line, Frank yelled out my time. I fell to my knees. My dad gave three loud claps. Frank made me get up and keep walking. I put my hands on my head, sucking in deep drags of air through my nose. It'd been seven months since the injury. I couldn't believe it.

On the morning of the actual mile race, with Stanford's campus again buzzing with students, none of my teammates knew I was going to participate. I didn't even tell my best friend and roommate I was going to run. They all asked, but I just said I'd have to see how it felt. I wasn't playing full-court basketball yet, so no one had any idea how I'd recovered. My parents didn't understand why I was keeping everyone in the dark. Neither did I, really.

The reason I did it, I now understand, was anger. I was angry that I didn't party with my teammates once all summer, that I sat in Anyu's apartment and iced my knee when my friends were out having fun, that I spent my time relearning how to walk instead of leaving school early and joining my dad as one of the only Jewish basketball players ever drafted into the NBA. I was angry that people viewed me as a privileged kid who never had to struggle for anything, even though I was precisely a privileged kid who never had to struggle for anything. I was angry that I was perceived as different, totally different, than my grandma and dad. My first head coach at Stanford, Mike Montgomery, had once wondered why I had such a chip on my shoulder. "What are you fighting for?" he asked as I sat in his office. "It's not like you're an immigrant like your dad."

My face burned when I heard that. I hated that he said it, and I hated that he was right. At Stanford, we had to wear team-issued gear to every workout. There were no exceptions. Our colors were red and white. I came to the track the morning of the mile race in all black — black shorts, a long-sleeve black T-shirt, black socks, and the black knee brace I'd worn all summer. My energy and my apparel both told the same story: I was back, and I was now a certified nutjob. None of the coaches said a word about my clothes, even though they broke a team rule. They could probably tell I wasn't in my right mind.

I could hear the hollers from my teammates as they saw me approaching the track. They ran over to pat my shoulders and to welcome me back. I smiled. I knew something they didn't. I started jogging to warm up. I could feel their eyes on me. No one had seen me run since the injury. They didn't know for sure if I even could run. When we were told to get on the starting line, I took the inside position. Teammates settled around me. My stomach was tingling. I tightened my knee brace, inhaled deeply, and closed my eyes. All I could hear were my teammates' short bursts of breath as we waited for the race to begin. I put my hand over my heart. Then, finally, our coach yelled "go."

I shot forward. My plan was to run my race and not worry about anyone else. I wanted to get into a rhythm for three laps and leave everything on the track for the fourth lap. I recall being in the lead at some points and dropping a few people back at others. My strides stayed steady, and my knee was pain free. Teammates would pass me up around a curve then wear down and fall behind. Starting the final lap, I was in the lead, and my teammates' feet were fading. As my arms pumped, my eyes stayed wide and still. My coaches were watching from outside the track. I think they were getting a sense of how I'd spent my summer. They, like Coach Montgomery, were probably wondering what the hell was wrong with me.

The truth was that I was under the spell of a legacy they knew nothing about. I was exactly the same as billions of other people in the world searching for belonging. It just so happened that I wanted to belong to a family story. I wanted hard work and resilience to apply to me, too.

The practice mile I'd run with my dad looking on was clocked at 5:25. When I crossed the line to win the official mile race, my coach yelled out a time of 5:10. It was five seconds slower than I'd run the year before. The first thing I did after winning the race was call my dad. "I won," I said when he picked up the phone.

"I knew you would," he replied.

I didn't survive the Holocaust and wasn't a rose that grew from concrete, but I could also persevere. I was starting to understand that everyone's triumph looks different.

chapter 12

death & basketball

I N THE SUMMER OF 1996, ANYU SET OFF ACROSS ITALY with my mom, sister, and maternal grandparents on a two-week trip of a lifetime. They visited the Colosseum in Rome. They floated down canals in Venice and toured the Duomo in Florence. They snapped pictures and took naps. Over fresh-baked bread and bottles of red, Anyu told jokes well into the night as the sun dipped and relented. Each morning, Anyu smoked my 15-year-old sister out of their shared room with a mustard cloud of Aqua Net hairspray. She ordered something with porcini mushrooms every night. They reminded her of a place that was beautiful and simple. It existed only in her mind.

Dad and I didn't get the invite to Italy. I was at summer camp in Wisconsin, where there were pine trees and jet skis and a crystal lake to skip rocks on. I could be found on the basketball courts. I was 12 and had just finished sixth grade. Dad was in New York signing basketball players. He was the general manager of the New York Knicks, and they had a lot of money to spend in free agency. His assistants would overnight press clippings to me at camp so I could follow the news. If I didn't know what was going on with the Knicks, I could barely fall asleep at night. When my envelope would arrive, I'd tear it open on my bed and read articles about NBA free agency from the *New York Daily News*, *USA TODAY*, or *Newsweek*. Kids in my cabin thought it was nuts. They had a point.

In Rome, my family stayed at The Excelsior, a luxurious hotel on Via Veneto, Rome's famous thoroughfare. The Excelsior was part of Sheraton's Luxury Collection, a group of high-end hotels owned by the owners of the Knicks. When Anyu checked into her room, there was a bottle of champagne and a plate of chocolates waiting for her. A card welcomed Mrs. Grunfeld as a VIP guest and thanked her for visiting The Excelsior. Anything she needed, the card said, she shouldn't hesitate to ask.

The first time Anyu had visited Via Veneto was when my family lived as refugees in Rome after fleeing Romania in 1963. A Jewish non-profit had paid for Anyu to take lessons on Via Veneto to become a hairdresser. She made friends with another refugee who'd been in Rome for a few months. When Anyu walked by The Excelsior for the first time with her friend on the way to their lesson, the friend grabbed her arm. "Make sure you don't sit in there," she said, pointing into the ornate lobby. "They will kick you out."

Now, they were calling her Mrs. Grunfeld. Anyu smiled and took a bite of her chocolate.

Anyu, Apu, Lutzi, and Dad lived in Rome from November 1963 until April 1964. They stayed on the fifth floor of 31 Via Montopoli, in a single room of an apartment owned by a Garibaldi, one of Italy's historic families. The landlord was called Signora. She was forced to rent out the room after her uncles had lost the majority of the family fortune betting on horses. Her dad had donated a massive diamond to the Italian government in more prosperous times, but Benito Mussolini had taken it for himself during the War. Signora was immediately drawn to the young Romanian boy who kissed his parents and gazed up at his brother. She bought Dad his first real toys, which offered more than the rocks, ropes, and cardboard boxes he'd played with in Romania.

In Rome, Dad and Lutzi kicked the soccer ball on the terrace, ate steaming ciriola bread at the local bakery, and took a cramped city bus to an Italian school. They visited St. Peter's Basilica and walked around the Vatican. They watched television at home. Like Romanian, Italian is a romance language, so Dad picked it up easily. It didn't take long for him to ask about the local soccer team, compliment Signora's pasta sauce, and request bigger shoes — all in proper Italian.

With her Israeli passport in hand, Anyu was excited about joining her sisters in Israel, but her brother Andy was in New York City. Everyone said America was where the opportunities were. Apu wanted to go to America. He'd heard about the streets paved with gold. My uncle Lutzi had been dating a girl in Romania who was moving to America, so he wanted to be in the United States, too. Anyu could say no to her husband; her son was a different story. They stayed in Rome as they learned more about coming to America.

Apu called HIAS, a non-profit organization that provides support and humanitarian aid to people whose lives and freedoms are at risk. Their slogan is: "Welcome the stranger. Protect the refugee." When my family was fleeing Romania, HIAS met their train as it stopped over in Belgrade and provided a much-needed free meal: a plate of spinach with an over-easy egg.

The people at HIAS indicated that they could get visas for America if given a few months. In the meantime, they took care of the paperwork and provided English tutors. Dad was fluent in Hungarian and Romanian and functional in Italian. He'd never met anyone who spoke English. *Ferris wheel, apple, school bus, fingernail, waterfall* — what kind of words were these?

When the visas were ready, HIAS paid for the flights to America with the understanding that the price of the tickets would be reimbursed when Apu and Anyu found work. On April 13, 1964, their Pan Am flight landed at JFK Airport. They stood on American soil for the first time, in New York City, the center of the universe, a long way from Auschwitz and communism and everything else. Dad had wings clipped to his shirt when he arrived at his Uncle Andy's apartment on Decatur Avenue in the Bronx. He spoke no English, as was the case with the rest of the family. At least the money from Buddy Hackett was waiting for them in the bedroom closet.

After spending a few months in the Bronx, Apu found an apartment in Forest Hills, Queens, on 75th Avenue between Austin Street and Queens Boulevard. Rent was $130 a month. The Buddy Hackett money helped. They could've paid half that in the Bronx, but the schools in Forest Hills were better. Anyu wanted the boys to get the type of education the War had denied her. Forest Hills was also a Jewish neighborhood, which didn't hurt.

The apartment was on the sixth floor, opposite a line of row houses. Since there were no tall buildings across the street, the living room got plenty of natural light. The apartment had one bedroom, one bathroom, a kitchenette with a table near the window, and a living room with a small television perched against the wall. A *mezuzah* — a sacred object used to mark the doorpost of a Jewish home — was affixed to the right side of the door. It'd been brought from Israel. It was a small metal strip with swirling blue dots. The Austin Street Playground was right around the corner from the apartment. The local school, PS101, was a half mile away. Anyu put two mattresses in the living room for the boys. After a few months of working and saving, she replaced the mattresses with a pullout couch. Dad and his brother slept on it together. Lutzi would kiss Dad on his head and say goodnight in Hungarian.

Outside the living room window at 111-15 75th Avenue, there were pockets of resistance forming in New York City. The Black community rioted in Harlem in '64 against police brutality after the cops shot and killed a 15-year-old Black boy. The Stonewall Riots in Manhattan in '69 would define the LGBTQ movement for decades. There would be strikes by the transit union and the teacher's union. A sanitation strike would leave trash uncollected for nine days.

Meanwhile, new immigration laws were turning New York City into a multicultural metropolis unlike any the world had seen. Senators Ted and Bobby Kennedy fought to pass the Hart-Celler Act in '65 to eliminate immigration quotas based on national origin, a policy that favored white people from Western Europe. Immigrants of different colors from different cultures would become the norm in America. The act was signed into existence on Liberty Island, in the heart of New York City, with the Kennedys in attendance. A few years later, Bobby Kennedy was assassinated. A young Palestinian man shot and killed the presidential hopeful because he supported Israel after the Six-Day War.

Two New York baseball teams had moved to California in the late '50s. The Dodgers had gone from Brooklyn to Los Angeles, and the Giants went from Manhattan to San Francisco. In 1962, the Mets came to New York. At first, they played at the Polo Grounds in Upper Manhattan, just north of Central Park, before moving into Shea Stadium in '64. Shea Stadium was in Queens, so Dad became a Mets fan.

The Knicks were at the bottom of the standings in '64, still playing at the old Madison Square Garden on 8th Avenue between 49th and 50th. They were a year away from drafting Willis Reed from Grambling and three years away from hiring Red Holzman, a Jew from Brooklyn, as their head coach. They'd move into the new Madison Square Garden, "The World's Most Famous Arena," between 7th and 8th Avenues from 31st to 33rd. They'd quickly bring New York City to its knees with two NBA championships. Red Holzman would become Dad's mentor, but not for a few decades. Dad had to learn English first.

Dad's first school in America was a yeshiva in the Bronx, a Jewish school that mixed secular education with instruction of ancient Jewish texts. The yeshiva was Orthodox, so there was school on

Sunday. Classes were taught in both English and Hebrew. Dad spoke neither. He was a third grader who was as big as a fifth grader, but since he couldn't communicate, he was put into class with the first graders. Among kids his own age, he was enormous. With the first graders, he looked like he should've been teaching the class.

When they moved into their place in Forest Hills, Anyu and Apu wanted Dad to go to Solomon Schechter, a yeshiva in Queens. Dad was ecstatic when he was denied admission. The stated reason was that he couldn't speak English. He enrolled instead as a fourth grader at PS101 and excelled in math, a universal language. Mrs. Kinkaid was patient with the oversized new boy from Europe who couldn't speak but wanted to. She'd have one of her best students sit with him in the back of the room during class and teach him how to read. He'd sound out words and look at pictures to understand what they meant. A kid named Ronnie was the main student who helped. Ronnie lived in the neighborhood right next to the Austin Street Playground, where everyone went to play basketball.

Outside of school, kids teased Dad because he didn't speak English. They'd shake their heads at him and mimic the strange sounds of his native Hungarian. They'd point to the other side of the street and signal for him to walk over there. When he'd cross the street and look back, they'd laugh at him and walk away. There were some Italians in the neighborhood, so Dad would speak their language with them. He mostly just sat in the apartment. On one of his early nights in Queens, Dad heard helicopter blades slapping overhead. He didn't think much of it. He had no idea that a band from the United Kingdom was landing less than a mile from his apartment for a concert at the tennis stadium in Forest Hills. Dad didn't know about the concert, nor had he heard of the band. It was The Beatles.

Apu got a job painting houses in Connecticut. Anyu worked as a floor girl in a T-shirt factory in Brooklyn, carrying unfinished shirts to the machines to be imprinted. Lutzi was 17 and a rising senior at Forest Hills High School. Girls flocked to his good looks and charm, even though his English was shaky. At least he could pronounce his American name: Leslie. When he could, my uncle would take Dad around the neighborhood with him, like he used to in Romania.

For entertainment, Anyu would give Dad a dollar so he could go to the local movie theater, even though he barely understood the words. Half the money could buy a children's ticket; the other half was meant for candy from the snack bar. The ushers at the theater thought Dad was far too large to be a kid. He had bigger feet than they did. He didn't know the language well enough to defend himself, so they charged him the full adult price for the ticket. He sat in the movie alone with no candy, trying to understand the plot without understanding the words.

After a few months in America, Dad's English improved, and a normal life in New York City looked possible. Then my uncle's legs started to bruise. All of a sudden, balls of blue and purple spotted his thighs, calves, and shins. There was never excessive contact during soccer to cause it, no falling while playing basketball worth mentioning, no acute incidents of any kind to produce this type of reaction. The bruises simply bubbled to the surface, sent from somewhere dark and deep, and they wouldn't stop coming.

Anyu couldn't speak the language well enough to bring Lutzi to the doctor by herself, so a friend accompanied her and did the talking. She explained the symptoms. The doctor's face was tight as he peered over clear spectacles at my uncle, who was sitting on a stiff plastic chair waiting to be examined. My uncle had copper skin, lean shoulders, and symmetrical features. He'd never heard the

English phrase "tall, dark, and handsome," but he was it. He was an All-American type who just happened to be Romanian.

The doctor placed his hands on my uncle's warm skin. He prodded his abdomen to assess the liver and spleen. He felt his glands. Eventually, he took his blood. As results were being analyzed on a subsequent visit, my uncle sat nonchalantly in the waiting room, his lengthy bruised legs crossed out in front of him. He hummed his favorite song, "Everybody Loves Somebody," by Dean Martin. He was too young and strong to let anything worry him. Anyu sat next to him. Her heart was hammering against her ribs. When the test results were explained, Anyu couldn't understand what the doctor was saying, but she knew how to read body language. As the doctor spoke, his English fast and foreign, Anyu was having a hard time catching her breath. Her friend translated into Hungarian — something about a problem with the blood — but she didn't go into detail. And she never said the word. Somehow, Anyu already knew. On the way home, she walked several feet in front of my uncle so he wouldn't see her shaking.

Anyu had a cousin from Budapest who was a prominent doctor at Long Island Jewish Medical Center, one of the best hospitals in Queens. He brought in a specialist to see my uncle. The specialist conducted the same type of exam as the first doctor with a few more tests and a more comprehensive blood panel. The specialist shared the results with Anyu's cousin, whose features hardened as he told Anyu the news in Hungarian.

He finally said the word: cancer. It was leukemia, and it was terminal.

At that moment, a piece of Anyu's heart drifted off, never to be seen again. The doctor gave her a Valium to handle the stress. She hugged her son and swallowed her tears. She then went home to tell Apu the worst news he had ever gotten — worse even than what had happened to his family in Auschwitz. They let Dad know that Lutzike was sick, but they didn't tell him the extent of it. They didn't tell my uncle the extent of it, either. How do you tell a little boy his big brother is going to die? How do you tell a young man he's going to die?

Desperate and delirious from her urge to protect her child, Anyu contacted the Hasidic Jew from Romania who used to sell her American dollars. He was close friends with Joel Teitelbaum, the famous rabbi from Satu Mare who'd left his congregation for Brooklyn during the War. He'd once blessed Anyu as a child in her parents' home. Now, she needed him to tell her that he could stop what was happening to her son. When Anyu relayed the message to Rabbi Teitelbaum through her old money dealer, the response she received from the rabbi was honest and heartbreaking. "I'm very sorry," the rabbi said, "but there is nothing either of us can do to stop this."

Lutzi spent weeks at a time in the hospital, so Anyu quit the new job she'd gotten at a watchband factory in Queens. She was by his bedside every day. My grandparents didn't have a car, so Anyu's cousin picked her up in the morning and dropped her off at night. Sometimes, when my uncle was scheduled for a blood transfusion, volunteers would take him and Anyu back and forth from the hospital. Apu continued to paint houses in Connecticut. They needed the money. As my uncle got thinner and weaker, the strokes of Apu's paint brush grew hurried and careless. As soon as he came home to Queens, his first stop was the hospital to visit his son. During those long hospital stays, Dad would live at his Uncle Andy's in the Bronx. He'd make occasional trips to the hospital to see his king.

When Lutzi would come home from the hospital, Dad would come home from the Bronx. They'd sleep in their bed together on the pullout couch in the living room. Anyu was 39 at the time. Her greatest joy in America had been watching out the window as my uncle put his arm around my dad and walked him into the neighborhood. Even the Holocaust couldn't prepare someone for this. Weeks before my uncle died, Anyu was by Lutzi's bedside. He must have sensed that he didn't have much time. "Anyu," he said, his voice sounding stronger than it had in months. "Can I tell you something?"

Anyu grabbed his hand. "Of course, Tatele," she said. "What is it?"

They were, as usual, speaking Hungarian. "My brother, Ernie," he said, his eyes wide. "There's nothing I would love more than for him to become a famous person in America."

Anyu nodded her head and gave him a kiss. Dad was nine at the time. He could barely have a conversation in English and hadn't yet touched a basketball. For the rest of her life, Anyu would wonder what had made Lutzi say what he said. My dad would have no idea, either. Maybe his brother understood that Dad had a gift he hadn't yet discovered. That's what I like to think, at least.

Dad's 10th birthday was on April 24, 1965. Three days later, early in the morning on April 27, my uncle started to bleed. They had stopped his medication two weeks prior. Anyu knew what was coming. "Ernie," she said in a rushed tone, "bring me a wet towel for Lutzike."

The request was her way of getting Dad out of the room. She didn't want him to see. She immediately called Andy, who came and brought Dad to his house in the Bronx. Dad kissed his brother good-bye like he did every time they parted. He didn't know it, but it would be the last time.

They contacted my grandpa in Connecticut and told him to get to the hospital right away. Apu made his trips to Connecticut by hitching rides with friends and coworkers. He didn't have access to an automobile, but he arrived at the hospital in no time. Anyu never found out how he got there so fast. My grandpa took that knowledge to his grave. Unfortunately, it wasn't fast enough. He didn't make it in time. He never got the chance to say good-bye to his son.

My uncle Leslie's funeral was at Schwartz Brothers Funeral Home in Queens, a year after the family had arrived in New York. He's buried at New Montefiore Cemetery on Long Island. While sick in the hospital, he wrote a letter to the girl he'd dated in Romania saying he one day wanted to move to California and pursue a career in film. He'd never get a chance to write his story in America. My dad's part would be improbable. I can't imagine what his big brother might have done.

My uncle's absence is a void that can't be filled. A generation later, the loss is haunting. My dad can't talk about him. Anyu can't look at his picture for long. I can't imagine. My middle name is Leslie, after him. I was given the name of someone sacred, and he lives inside of me. He is a part of me. I carry his name, so my success is his success. My dreams are his dreams. Whenever I can, I go out of my way to tell people my middle name. It gives me a chance to talk about my uncle. I want to make sure people know he existed.

I've never had the courage to ask my dad if, as a player for the New York Knicks, he visited Lutzi's grave to tell him that his little brother had become that famous person in America after all. For whatever reason, I don't want to know the answer.

chapter 13

an accident & Larry Bird

THE 2006 NBA DRAFT WAS HELD ON JUNE 28 AT THE Theatre at Madison Square Garden in New York City. My family had sat in the first row there every year to see a live performance of *A Christmas Carol* when my dad was running the Knicks. I watched the draft from my agent's house in Los Angeles as guys who I'd outplayed the year I got injured became NBA players and millionaires. I dropped the remote on the couch and went to the gym to work out. I knew no one would pick me.

I'd won the mile race and posted 29 points and nine rebounds in the first game of my senior year at Stanford, but my recuperating body couldn't withstand a full college basketball schedule. My mind couldn't, either. The brace on my right knee was a constant reminder of the injury, and I was a half-step slow, a dangerous limitation for someone with zero margin for error when it came to speed. As the season wore on, I began to ask Anyu if I could spend a night or two at her apartment during the week just to get a break. I'd eat *faschilt* and *piros krumpli* and try not to think about basketball. By the end of the season, my scoring average had plummeted right along with my draft stock.

On the way to the gym on draft night, I called my dad. He told me to keep my head up and keep working. I'd been through something traumatic, he said, and this was just the beginning of a long career for me. He told me to be patient and stay positive. I listened, but it was not supposed to be this way. This was fucking bullshit.

After going undrafted, I accepted an offer to play NBA Summer League with the Indiana Pacers. Summer league was a chance for free agents like me to spend a week playing organized games to prove we belonged in the NBA. It'd been a year and a half since my injury. I was almost fully healed, finally, but my window was still small. I could outwork people, but I wasn't as naturally gifted of an athlete as my pro competition, especially while recovering from something so severe. I saw limited minutes with the Pacers and was completely unremarkable. A few games into summer league, it became clear that I'd start my pro career in Europe. I'd never been to Europe and didn't know much about it — aside from my family being from there. The notion of living and playing basketball abroad made my stomach burn. I'd grown up in the NBA. I was an American. Playing in Europe was literally and figuratively a foreign concept.

My only accomplishment during my introduction to the pro ranks at NBA Summer League was that I was once and for all able to prove the profound depths of my love for basketball. It happened off the court and was an appropriate representation of a pro career that was not quite starting off as I'd envisioned. If there was ever an argument that the game could only push me to do so much, I laid that argument to rest at summer league. It's hard to believe that it was Larry Bird, one of my childhood heroes, that provided me with the opportunity.

It's fair to say that I'd been conditioned since birth to worship Larry Bird. When I was born in February of 1984, Larry Bird was the best basketball player on the planet. Bird's Boston Celtics were sitting atop the standings in the East the day of my birth. Bird was months away from posting 39 points, 12 rebounds, and 10 assists in Game 7 of the Eastern Conference Semifinals as the Celtics eliminated my dad's Knicks team from the playoffs. Bird would lead the Celtics to the NBA title that year. He'd be named league MVP, Finals MVP, and first-team All-NBA. He even made the NBA All-Defensive second team, an egregious accolade for a guy with the lateral quickness of an elevator.

Growing up, I'd pester my dad for stories about the best players he ever went up against in the NBA. Bird's name would always be at the top of the list. Dad and I would sit at the kitchen table as he talked about how big and crafty Bird was, about the trash he talked. He'd tell me about how Bird would dip his shoulder, take two slow dribbles, and raise up to shoot effortlessly over Dad's defense. The shot would go in, and Bird's elbow would slam into Dad's face as he was completing his shot. The refs would usually call a foul — on my dad. "I guess my face used to get in the way of his elbow," was Dad's response. "No one could guard Larry Bird, including me." He'd pause a second. "Especially me."

At the peak of Bird's dominance, the NBA was a predominantly Black league — the majority of NBA players were Black, and there'd only been two white MVPs since 1959 — yet here was a 6'9" guy from French Lick, Indiana with floppy hair, pasty legs, and unstoppable basketball ability. Everything about Bird's brilliance defied convention. Before starting at Indiana State University, he'd been employed as a garbage collector in his hometown. He spent his days on the street picking up trash. On the court, as my dad remembered all too well, he spent his time talking it. As a Celtics great, he became a cultural icon, a symbol that it doesn't matter what you look like or where you come from. I admired Larry Bird before I could even say Larry Bird. Dad always hated the Celtics, but he respected No. 33.

Given Bird's mythological stature in my life, it's not hard to predict how I responded to the following question when I was asked it at NBA Summer League, 22 years after Bird's dominance in 1984: "Dan, Larry is having some of the guys for dinner tonight. Would you like to join?"

I was lying on the floor of the gym stretching my hamstring after practice. Larry Bird was the general manager of the Pacers, but this was still the last thing I expected to hear. The question was asked by the Pacers' equipment manager, Corky, a short bald guy who'd been with Larry since Boston. *Dinner with Larry Freaking Bird? Are you kidding me? Who in their right mind says no to that?* Not me. Not then. Not now. Not ever. "Yeah, that'd be great," I said as I switched legs, trying to sound casual because 22 year olds think it's cool not to care about anything even if they're secretly flipping out inside. "Just text me the time and place."

A few hours after practice, as I was napping, I got the info from Corky. "Mo's. 7:00."

Mo's was a steakhouse on Maryland Street in Indianapolis, a 10-minute walk from our hotel. I could feel my shoulders tingle with anticipation. *Oh man*, I thought. *I'm eating dinner with Larry Bird tonight.* I tried to stay calm, but it was Larry Bird. The championship in '84. Sixty points against the Atlanta Hawks in '85. The championship in '86. An entire childhood talking hoops with my dad.

Bird had greeted me on the first day of practice for summer league, but that was the extent of our interaction. This was a whole dinner. A whole dinner with Larry Bird. This was a lot to deal with. I'd been living out of a suitcase for a week, wearing basketball shorts, T-shirts, and flip flops, so I rummaged through my bag to find the most presentable outfit I had. I went with a pair of baggy jeans, a bright yellow polo shirt, and a pair of Nike running shoes. It wasn't my best offering, but I did what I could with it.

On the walk to dinner, I tried to slow my stride to a reasonable pace. There were about 15 players on my summer league team. I hadn't talked about dinner with any of them and wasn't sure how many guys Corky had invited. I assumed that most of the team would be there, but I hadn't waited around the lobby to find out. Instead, I made the intentional choice to walk to dinner alone. My goal was to get to the restaurant 10 minutes early, before anyone else arrived, so I could scout out the seating and place myself close to Bird. If there were going to be a dozen guys or more at dinner, I didn't want to get stuck at the other end of the table from the legend.

When I reached the restaurant, I took a deep breath and swung open its double doors. As my beat-up Nikes carried me across the threshold, I was surprised to see that I wasn't the first one to arrive. Larry Bird and Corky were already sitting at a table not far from the entrance. I made eye contact with Bird. He waved me over. A chill shot up my spine. On my way to the table, my pulse was making its best attempt to jump out of my neck, not only because I was walking toward Larry Bird, but also because I saw that he and Corky were sitting at a table for four. Not 15. Not 10. Four. *Oh boy.*

After shaking hands and shuffling into my seat next to Bird, I grabbed my ice water to take a long gulp. The water was crisp and comforting. I downed it quickly. I thought of the many nights as a kid I'd stayed up late in my bed to read books about Larry Bird. Now, I was sitting right next to the man. I couldn't wait to tell my dad about this. As we began chatting, the sweat on my brow started to dry. My teammate Taylor Coppenrath, a former star at the University of Vermont, joined as our fourth. Naturally, our conversation revolved around basketball. Bird told stories about Magic Johnson, Moses Malone, LeBron James. My eyes bulged. *What a night.* I remember ordering food at some point, but I don't remember what. To cool my nerves, I worked that water like my life depended on it. I changed the subject from hoops right as our food was set down. "So Larry," I said, "you golf much?"

I had never and have never played a round of golf, but I felt like this was the type of question a guy would ask Larry Bird as they broke bread at a steakhouse. So I asked it. "Not too often," Bird said, "I enjoy it but don't do it enough."

"How's your game?" I asked.

"All right," he said. "I'm about a three handicap."

I shook my head. I knew that pros were generally scratch golfers, meaning they hovered around a zero handicap. At a three handicap, Larry Bird was at the level of a semipro, without playing much. I smiled and took another deep drag of ice water. This was about the time of the night when the four or five glasses of water started to catch up to me. The pressure in my bladder began to mount. The feeling of having to go to the bathroom settled like a moist cloud, but I was sitting next to Larry Bird. My childhood had been spent dreaming of a moment like this. I pushed the burning sensation to the back of my mind. I loved basketball far too much even to consider excusing myself from the table. How does one cut off a conversation with Larry Bird? My dad had raised me better than that. I'd hold the pee. It wasn't an emergency.

By the time the dessert plates were cleared, my eyes had begun to lose focus. The pain in my bladder was now searing, but the check would be coming soon, and I was healthy and strong. I'd say a proper good-bye to Bird then head straight to the bathroom. I just couldn't excuse myself. I was with a childhood icon. I empathize with my 22-year-old self. I understand why I stayed at the table and continued to down ice water despite the heaviness in my abdomen. "Let's go grab the car," Larry Bird said after he'd paid the bill.

The sensation had turned white hot. I should've just separated from the group to use the restroom. In my mind, though, "grabbing the car" implied that Larry Bird might be dropping me and my teammate off at the hotel. That was not a ride I was prepared to jeopardize. I followed the group out of the restaurant and walked a minute to Bird's Mercedes. "Thanks for coming tonight," he said, extending his hand toward me. That hand was responsible for more than 20,000 NBA points. I gave it the firmest shake I could. That hand was humongous.

"Thanks for having me," I said with a crooked smile.

Larry Bird and Corky slid into the car and sped away. My evening with the legend was finished, and it'd been euphoric. So euphoric, in fact, that I believe it temporarily rewired my cerebral cortex. Instead of telling my teammate about my dire situation so I could find a bathroom and deal with it, I just started walking with him toward the hotel. I inexplicably said nothing. I was drunk on Larry Bird, and I'd never had to pee so badly in my life. With that first step toward the hotel, I'd made a commitment. I'd hold it for the 10-minute walk. There were likely a dozen places I could've stopped on the way back, but I was on autopilot. My head was hazy with the sound of Larry Bird's soft Indiana twang bouncing around my brain like a sweeping lefty hook off the glass.

My teammate made small talk as we progressed toward the hotel. I wasn't listening and couldn't engage. All systems were occupied. When I eventually saw the hotel a few blocks away, my eyes grew large. When the lobby's sweet scent hit my nostrils, my spirits soared. *I'm gonna make it.* The pain was now overwhelming, but our wait for the elevator was mercifully short. Writhing and wiggling, I stepped in and pressed the button for my floor. My teammate pushed his. It was below mine. *Damn it. More time to wait.*

As we ascended the floors, I stood frozen in place, sweat accumulating on my forehead. I was blatantly ignoring my teammate. When he reached his floor, I waved a quick good-bye. I was finally alone, climbing toward sweet relief. *Just a little longer.* When my floor dinged and the doors slid open, I burst into the hallway. My room was two doors down from the elevator. My heart was pounding. My chest was tight with panic. I was barely hanging on and couldn't orient myself. There was too much happening.

I instinctively made a left out of the elevator, searching for my room. *Where is it? Where the hell is it?* Unfortunately, my room was to the right of the elevator, not the left. I'd tilted off my axis and had lost all ability to make sense of my surroundings. Spinning circles in the hallway, scanning furiously for my room, I knew there was only one end in sight. To put it simply, I'd reached the point of no return. As my eyes darted and my body pivoted, the floodgates began to open, right there in the hallway. *It's happening. Oh my God, it's happening.*

There's something very strange about peeing yourself as an adult. There's a surreal quality to the experience. Shame, self-loathing, and astonishment were present, certainly, but it wasn't all negative. The release was strangely liberating. The pain finally had an outlet. The beast no longer controlled me. A few seconds of peeing yourself feels like an eternity. It was all I needed to lower the pressure and regain my bearings. I realized where my room was and bolted toward it. I fumbled my way inside, ripped off my belt, and located the toilet.

When it was over, I stood in the silent bathroom, breathless, exhausted, and relieved. I looked at myself in the mirror. My face was red, my brow glistening. I tried and failed to look myself in the eyes. I called my mom. "How was dinner with Larry Bird?" she asked.

"It was amazing," I said. "Dad would've loved it. Also, how do you clean pee off jeans?"

She was not as surprised by this question as I would've liked her to be. She laughed for several minutes before giving me instructions. She insisted I call the rest of the family to tell them what'd happened. Dad was more interested in Bird than the pee story. "Did he talk about our series in '84?" he asked.

My sister nearly peed herself listening to how stubbornly I'd refused to get up from the table. "*Oy vey,*" Anyu said after I shared the news with her. "Don't feel bad, Tatele."

On the other end of the phone, I could hear her chuckling quietly.

It wasn't how I expected my professional basketball career to start, but I wouldn't change a thing about that dinner. The 10-year-old version of myself, the one that ran around Madison Square Garden and shared basketball dreams with my dad, would have never, ever removed himself from a table occupied by Larry Bird. I know one thing for sure: that kid would've been damn proud.

chapter 14

the store & a beating

W HEN APU TOOK MY DAD TO THE CIRCUS AT
Madison Square Garden, Anyu stayed home. When the
World's Fair visited Queens from 1964 to 1965, promising a future
filled with flying cars and robotic laborers, Anyu told the boys to go
on without her. She'd be in her room, lights off, TV on. She didn't
want to see friends or take English lessons. She wouldn't accept gifts
or condolences. She wouldn't accept anything.

During the Holocaust, it was economic depression and blind
hatred that resulted in the murder of millions. A boy dying from
cancer just as his life was starting? There were no words to explain
that. Dad was sitting in the kitchen two years after my uncle had
died, watching the adults play rummy, when someone cracked a
joke. His face bent with surprise. *"Anyu,"* he said, *"mosolyogsz."*

In English, that translated to, "Mom, you're smiling." It was the
first time he'd seen it since his brother had passed.

The doctors wanted Dad to go back to school right away after
it happened. They said a regular schedule helps kids feel safe while
dealing with a tragedy, that it builds resilience and toughness. Dad's
king was gone, but there was life after loss. My grandparents knew
that from the War. They tried their best to convince Dad it was
true. When they tucked him in every night on the pullout couch
he'd once shared with his brother, they tried their best to convince
themselves it was true.

Dad made an effort not to cry about his brother. Three weeks
after Lutzi died, Anyu returned to the job she'd left at the watchband
factory in Queens. They needed the money. Every morning, she
took the subway to the factory on Norton Avenue. Several hundred

people, mostly immigrants, worked in the gray stone building. Some of them spoke Hungarian, but the main mode of communication was broken English. A Jewish man from Poland owned the factory. He paid Anyu $80 a week — twice as much as she'd made at the T-shirt factory in Brooklyn when they first got to America. He came by and patted her shoulder once she settled back in after the funeral. He said he was sorry.

With her eyes narrow and her breath deliberate, Anyu made watch after watch. The honest day's work helped occupy her mind. When the Polish factory owner needed three workers to fashion gold bands instead of the ordinary metal ones, Anyu was the first person selected. Her colleagues couldn't comprehend her sense of purpose at work. That was fine with her.

Apu stopped painting houses in Connecticut and became a leather coat cutter in Manhattan. He worked at the same factory as Anyu's brother, Andy. Apu wasn't good with his hands like Anyu, but if he could figure out how to be a cook in a Hungarian labor camp during the Holocaust, he could cut leather in New York City.

My grandparents were determined to build on the leftover Buddy Hackett money. They made sure what came in exceeded what went out. Their biggest splurge was stopping at Howard Johnson's on Wednesday nights after work for the all-you-can-eat buffet. Just $1.19 a person got them a bottomless plate of fish and chips with unlimited coleslaw on the side. Anyu swears the fish was excellent. She was likely just very hungry.

After a half year working long days and enjoying fish pulled from the murky shallows of the Hudson River, Apu took the Buddy Hackett money and what they'd added to it since arriving in America and found a partner, who was also from Romania. Together, they opened up a fabric store in the Bronx. It was on Tremont Avenue, in between a pet store and a clothing outlet and across the street from a movie theater. Apu and his partner put in $5,000 each to get the store up and running. As soon as Apu saw that the store could be profitable, he bought out his partner for $15,000. His first move was to bring on Anyu full time. She was upset at first to leave her friends at the watch factory, but she quickly fell in love with Tremont Fabrics. It was theirs.

Anyu worked at the store six days a week, and Apu worked seven. On Sundays, with the store closed, he'd take their new station wagon to Manhattan or New Jersey to buy fabric. Anyu cooked and cleaned all day to prepare for the week. Their clientele in the Bronx was low income, mostly Black and Hispanic. Fabric was in high demand, since their customers sewed their own clothes to save money. The store carried fabrics in most materials and patterns, in addition to curtains, furniture covers, trimmings, thread, zippers, seam binding, hair ribbons, and other accessories.

Apu was the salesman and buyer while Anyu made fabric suggestions and ran the register. She picked up Spanish to communicate with their customers. She wasn't good with faces and had a hard time remembering the regulars. When the door opened, Apu would whisper the customer details under his breath in Hungarian. *Corduroy, bright colors, patterns. Name is Robert.* The store was so busy that they regularly missed lunch at the local luncheonette. On slower days, Anyu went and brought food back for them. The harder they worked, the less time they had to think.

On his parents' orders, Dad took the subway to the Bronx to work at the store each Saturday. He'd ride the E train from 75th Avenue into the city, transferring at the 7th Avenue station to the D train toward the Bronx. He'd get off at Grand Concourse then walk a mile to Tremont Fabrics. Despite his young age, he was big and broad enough that nobody thought to bother him on the streets of New York.

Walking into the store, Dad was swept up by the rush of people. They were inspecting the big fabric spools lining the perimeter or rifling through the small rack of threads, needles, and zippers near the entrance. Up and down the middle of the store, shoppers flipped through books of patterns and referenced drawers stuffed with yards of fabrics. Lines formed at the measuring counter and cash register beyond the small rack to the right of the door. Anyu and Apu whizzed in and out of the fray, answering questions and corralling the traffic. They'd both run to give Dad a kiss as soon as he entered. Then they'd put him to work.

People did their shopping on Saturday, so it was the busiest day of the week. Dad's job was to make sure nobody stole anything. Spools of thread, clusters of needles, and tiny fabric patterns disappeared easily. Small items could be slipped in a pocket or purse with little effort. Dad would diligently stand watch over that section of the store. He wanted people to know that there'd be consequences and repercussions for stepping out of line. Ultimately, he never caught anyone stealing. He was either really good at his security job or really bad at his security job.

Once in a while, his parents let him operate the cash register for fun. Overall, he dreaded those Saturdays. All the other kids were out in the neighborhood playing sports. That's where he wanted to be. During the week, Dad was a latchkey kid, typical of immigrant children of the era. My grandparents were at the store from 8:00 AM to 8:00 PM, so he locked up the apartment when he left for elementary school in the morning and let himself in when he got home in the afternoon. He wore the house key on a thin string that hung around his neck. He walked to and from PS101 in Queens. The only rule was that, as soon as he got home from school, he had to call the store. "Anyu, I'm home," he'd say in Hungarian, "but I have to go to the bathroom." He always called before he peed. He took the rule seriously.

Dad's English was improving, but he'd never be a native speaker. When kids on the street bragged about the burgers and pizza they'd had for dinner, his tales of *ciorba* and *uborkasaláta* didn't bring the house down. He was only a few years removed from communism, silently trying to tape over the hole in his heart left by his brother's death. When Lutzi died, so did Dad's direction. He spent most of his time in the empty apartment. As a lonely and disadvantaged immigrant, he was an at-risk youth in America. He needed to find something to be a part of. It didn't matter what. Just something productive. Kids in New York City who were in his position — different, wounded, and alone — turned to drugs, violence, gangs, or all three. For Dad, he just wanted to find friends. To fit in, he did like the other kids in the neighborhood: he went to the local park to play basketball.

He learned that the Austin Street Playground, as the park was named, was the social hub of the community. Dad saw New York City happening in every direction. Cars honked, babies cried, people fought, balls bounced. A chain-link fence surrounded the park. The Long Island Rail Road ran parallel, adding train whistles to the urban symphony, its wheels rumbling past day and night carrying weary travelers from the city to the island. The park had one full blacktop basketball court and another side hoop. Three basketball hoops total. There were swings and slides, courts for paddle ball and handball, tables and benches, some monkey bars. There was no grass. It was all concrete.

The jocks played basketball, touch football, stickball with a broom handle, street hockey with community sticks and a tennis ball, or games like "Johnny on the Pony," a park favorite. Dad once tried to explain the rules to me but gave up almost instantly. Based on the name alone, it sounded like a good time. The greasers at the park smoked cigarettes, did drugs, and talked shit. Guys played cards. Girls jumped rope. Vietnam vets with glassy eyes leaned on the fence. There were needles on the ground in the mornings from the junkies at night.

Under communism in Romania, Dad had never touched a basketball. Like his father, he played soccer and Ping-Pong, but basketball was religion in New York. It was the city game. It was the rhythm of the streets. Pee Wee Kirkland, Jumpin' Joe Hammond, and other New York City playground legends were celebrities in the five boroughs. New York had St. John's University, Rucker Park, the New York Knicks. The heart of the game of basketball beat in New York, since the city and the game shared undeniable similarities.

Like New York City, basketball for my dad was gritty and beautiful. The game required little space and no equipment, perfect for New York. It could be played individually or with two people, five people, 10 people, whatever. Money was not required. Only heart and hustle. Techniques were artistic and movements were graceful. There was a sense of expression to every player and every play. There was substance, style, and the interplay between the two.

Basketball was a game of communication, but players didn't need to speak the same language. Glances, gestures, and feelings dictated the flow of the game. Hungarian, English, German, Yiddish, Japanese — it was all the same on the court. Even a laundry basket and a crumpled T-shirt could spark a love for basketball. A milk crate and an empty jug could start a flame. A hoop and a ball could blaze in the right hands. To Dad, the game just happened to make sense. For whatever reason, it just clicked.

Playing basketball at the park helped him keep his mind off his brother. In the process, he made friends and learned English. The park also taught him physical toughness. Games were 3-on-3 to seven points, and the winner stayed on. A loss sent you to the back of the line. There were usually 50 or more kids waiting to play. It could take hours to get back on the court, so every possession mattered. If you got pushed around, you couldn't win, and winning was the only way to keep having fun.

Blocks away from the park, on the corner of Austin Street and Ascan Avenue, was Our Lady Queen of Martyrs, a Catholic school. When basketball season started, they needed a big kid to play on their fifth-grade CYO team. Though CYO stood for Catholic Youth Organization, they allowed two non-Catholic players on the team. Dad was offered one of the spots. It was his first organized basketball experience. He was the lone Jewish immigrant. He was inhaling plates of Anyu's *rántott hús* and *faschilt* by that point, so he had enough size to grab some rebounds and throw his body around. The games took place in the winter and were held at Ascension, a Catholic school on Grant Avenue off Queens Boulevard. Dad would take the Q60 bus to get there. Anyu and Apu would be at the store. They knew he was playing basketball, and he'd occasionally come home with a trophy, but they'd never seen him play before. They had no idea he ended up making the CYO All-Star team that first year, even though he was just learning the game.

As his basketball skills and English progressed, he felt more comfortable in his new country. Still, he could never completely shake the feeling of being an outsider, a European in America, a boy without a place. If he wanted to belong in the neighborhood, it had to happen at the park. On a hot summer day at the park weeks after sixth grade let out, Dad had a chance to prove himself when he and his new American friends were playing hoops on the blacktop. During a particular 3-on-3 game, Dad was matched up against a neighborhood kid named Billy, whose younger brother was one of

Dad's classmates. Billy had started high school already, so despite Dad's enormity for his age, Billy was the biggest guy on the court.

He took advantage of his stocky build by pushing around the younger boys, bullying his way to the basket with elbows bared. Dad could've earned a reputation by outplaying a high school kid at such a young age, but Billy was too strong and too mean. When he scored, he'd taunt the grade schoolers. When he felt like it, he'd spit wads of phlegm onto the pavement. At one point, Billy got tied up under the basket with Dad's friend, Mark, a scrawny sixth grader with matzo balls for shoulders. Pissed off, Billy grabbed the basketball and hurled it into Mark's stomach. Mark doubled over onto his knees, gasping for air, as Billy sneered and told him to kiss his ass. Mark eventually used all his strength to push himself off the ground. He walked off the court, his eyes locked on the concrete. The game was ruined. It wasn't uncommon for scuffles to break out at the park. Everyone went their separate ways.

Later in the day, Dad and his friends were still at the park, walking along the fence. Right outside the fence sitting on some parked cars were Billy and his crew. There were five or six of them. All high school aged, they wore greasy shirts and frayed shorts. My dad's friend Ronnie, the boy who'd sat with Dad in the back of the classroom and taught him how to sound out words like "sneaker" and "basket" when he'd just arrived in America, was little compared to the high school kids, but he was a New Yorker. One word he never taught Dad was "fear." "Hey, Billy, what the fuck is your problem?" Ronnie yelled in the direction of the older boys. "Real fucking tough picking on Mark like that."

Billy cocked his head. "Go fuck yourself, Ronnie," he said.

They started jawing back and forth. Dad was mild mannered and hadn't yet mastered the art of the American curse word, so he simply stood there and observed the spat. Eventually, Ronnie nudged his elbow. "Say something, Ernie," Ronnie said as things escalated, keenly aware that Dad was the only one close to the size of the older guys.

Dad didn't want to get involved, but Ronnie had taught him how to read. When other kids were making fun of him, Ronnie was helping with his vowels and telling him not to get discouraged. Dad dug deep and fired off the best thing he had in his arsenal: "Pick on someone your own size, Billy!" Dad shouted at their new rival in accented English.

Despite the insult lacking any respectable level of bite or ingenuity, it landed. Billy's eyes glowed. "Fuck you, Ernie!" Billy screamed. "If you want some, come get it."

That's all it took.

Billy and his friends jumped off the cars and made their way forward. Dad and his friends balled their fists and hurried around the gate. The groups tangled. Billy rushed Dad and threw him stomach first to the hot pavement. Billy put his knees on Dad's back, pinning him down. Dad tried to wrestle his way off the ground. He was the biggest sixth grader at the park, but he was no match for a high school kid. Billy's friends held the smaller boys at bay as Billy grabbed the back of Dad's head and started smashing his face into the concrete. Dad's skull bounced off the blacktop like a basketball. "Oh, shit!" Dad's friend yelled. "Get the hell off him!"

Dad's forehead slapped off the pavement five or six times before his friends could pull Billy off. They threw some thin punches as Billy backed away. When Dad stood up, his heart racing and his vision spiraling, blood ran down his face. He didn't have the wits to think how things would've gone if his brother were still around to protect him.

Billy and his crew backpedaled for an instant then hurried out of the park. Dad's friends made sure he was okay, then they also left the park together. Once they reached the neighborhood, Dad's buddies patted his back as they parted. Dad didn't say a word about what had happened. He'd see Billy again. And he wouldn't forget.

In the meantime, with the blood on his face already dried, Dad let himself into the apartment. All the lights were off. Anyu and Apu were still working at the store. In complete silence, he cleaned himself in the sink. He certainly didn't cry. That faucet had been turned off.

chapter 15

Germany now & then

WHEN I LANDED IN AMSTERDAM WITH MY MOM A few months after graduating from college, it was the first time I'd been in Europe. Every second person I saw in the airport was speaking a new language. The air smelled like coffee and croissants. Announcements echoed with words I didn't understand. I saw a toddler talking in Russian and was embarrassed by how impressed I was. The sounds of the people, their features, their gestures — it was all unfamiliar. Almost everyone was different, not just from me but from each other. I'd never seen heterogeneity at this scale before. My eyes were crooked from the transcontinental flight, but my heart raced at the promise of this new world.

We had a layover in Amsterdam before our flight to Germany, so I convinced my mom to visit the airport casino with me. It was early, but not too early to play a few hands of blackjack. I'd never seen a casino in an airport before, not even in Las Vegas. Europe, baby. Europe.

There was a man from Albania sitting at the blackjack table when we arrived. He was bald and stout with a stubbly beard and a cigarette perched behind his ear. As he leaned toward the dealer and muttered what had to be Albanian expletives, his butt crack peeked above the waistband of his gray sweatpants. I loved Europe already. I slapped down a hundred Euro bill and got 10 chips in return. My first hand was a solid 19. The dealer pulled a 20. My second hand was a solid 20. The dealer pulled a 21. I lost nine straight hands, keeping my last chip as a souvenir. For some reason, I had a great feeling about this whole Europe thing. Mom put her arm around my waist as we walked to the gate.

In 1932, the Nazis received 48.4 percent of the regional vote in Oldenburg, making it the first state in Germany to put the Nazis in power based on electoral turnout. When my agent called me excitedly to let me know that my best offer to start my pro career had come from the team in Oldenburg, in Germany's top league, I was unable to share his excitement. I told him I needed to talk to my grandma before I could make a decision. That was probably the first time he'd heard that from a pro basketball player. "Anyu," I said when she answered my call. "I have a good opportunity in Europe."

"*Mazel Tov*, Tatele," she said. "That's wonderful."

"There's a problem," I said. "It's in Germany."

As an elderly woman, Anyu became eligible to receive reparations from the German government, a monthly reminder of what had happened. She tried to ignore the deposit on her bank statement. Her parents and five siblings had been murdered. She got $275 a month in return. I had no idea how she'd react to the possibility of me living in Germany. I held my breath, but she didn't miss a beat. "What's the problem?" she asked.

"I thought you might be upset."

"Tatele," she said, "sons are not responsible for the sins of their fathers. I'm very proud of you."

I exhaled. "Thank you, Anyu," I said.

With Anyu's blessing, I started my career in Oldenburg, in northwest Germany, roughly 300 kilometers from the Netherlands, 500 kilometers from Denmark, and 1,200 kilometers from Budapest. I'd signed a one-year contract with the EWE Baskets Oldenburg, a respected team in Germany's Basketball Bundesliga. EWE, a German utilities conglomerate, was our main sponsor. The team provided me with a Peugeot SUV, a furnished two-bedroom apartment, health benefits, and $7,500 a month in salary after taxes. If not for my knee, I thought I'd be making millions in the NBA. With

$7,500 a month to burn with no expenses, I didn't understand how good I had it.

My new team put my mom and me up in our own hotel rooms on our first night in Oldenburg. It was a weekend in the early fall. The hotel was located in the city center. I was wide awake at 4:00 AM, jetlagged and unable to ignore the music pumping from the bars and clubs below. I grabbed the remote control off the nightstand and examined its unfamiliar shape. It was narrow and curved with big buttons and funny words on its face. It was unlike any remote I'd seen. I turned on the TV and flipped through the public channels. On one of the first stations, I saw a group of topless women pillow fighting. I lingered for 10 seconds. They usually charged for channels like that in the States.

When I turned off the TV and glanced out the window onto the cobblestone street below, my eyes flashed. I grabbed my sweatshirt and cell phone and was riding the elevator down before I realized why. The air was crisp as I made my way through the hotel doors. I looked around and saw kids sitting on the sidewalk eating pizza. A drunk couple was making out against a nearby wall. Friends were slapping each other's asses and running away. I was pleased to see this was a timeless pastime among buddies on every continent.

All around me, Germans maneuvered in and out of the many nighttime establishments lining the street. They were carrying liquor freely from one bar to another. That was not allowed in the States. I could see strobe lights flashing from the main club in the center of the action. This looked nothing like the Germany I'd heard about growing up. I called my dad, who was awake at home. He had trouble hearing me with all the partying in the background, so I shouted into the phone to describe the scene. When he replied, his voice was full. He told me how happy he was for me. He told me this would be a great experience for me. Eventually, he told me to take my ass back to bed.

The German first-division basketball league was made up of 18 teams, all located in West Germany. East German cities didn't have the infrastructure for a top team, since communism had left their economies decades behind. Over the course of the season, I traveled all across West Germany, bussing with my teammates to our road games. Our bus trips were sometimes 12 or 14 hours long. The bus usually had a bathroom in the back, but I kept an empty plastic water bottle in my bag at all times, just in case. After my Larry Bird incident, I could never be too safe.

When we played in Nuremberg, our team bus took a detour before practice to drive by the grounds of the Nuremberg Rallies, large Nazi propaganda events held in the 1930s. More than a million Germans attended the yearly event, which featured parades, processions, and speeches celebrating the Nazi cause. Anyu and her family were still in Micula at the time, blissfully unaware of what was coming. As the team bus rolled by the rally grounds, which have been preserved by Nuremberg officials as a reminder of the country's past, one of our German coaches pointed out the platform that Adolf Hitler had stood on to address the crowd. I stared at it and shook my head. I couldn't believe that man had stood right there. It hadn't been that long ago, either.

On a trip to play in Berlin, our team visited the Memorial to the Murdered Jews of Europe. It was in this city that World War II had ended after the Russians overcame the Germans in the Battle of Berlin, in May 1945. My grandparents were both back in Romania by then. Auschwitz had been liberated months prior. The Russians had already taken Raoul Wallenberg, who'd never be seen again. I walked silently through the maze of gray stone pillars of varying heights that made up the main section of Berlin's Holocaust memorial. These outdoor pillars were designed to produce feelings of disorientation and confusion for those who moved through them. They were intended to simulate the sensation of being trapped. As I turned corner after corner and found more of the same gray stone staring down at me, I felt small and alone.

My teammates knew I was close with my grandma. They had no idea that she'd survived the Holocaust or that my family members were among the murdered Jews of Europe. I was the only Jew on the team, and I may have been the only Jew in the league. Religion was not something I really talked about. The rest of my American teammates were joking within an hour of leaving the memorial, but I had problems sleeping that night. My mind was somewhere dark.

After visiting the memorial, my closest friend on the team, a German from Berlin, told me about the shame his generation felt for what their ancestors had done. He talked about how scared he'd been to see Germans gathering in large crowds and waving the flag when Germany won the soccer World Cup that summer in 2006. Public displays of nationalism had always been highly discouraged in his homeland, bordering on forbidden. He'd only seen a mob of Germans waving the flag in old black-and-white videos. He carried his history just like I carried mine.

I'd call Anyu from Germany every Sunday. I'd update her on my latest game and ask her why the German food was so heavy and bland. They also breaded and fried chicken, I'd say, but their *schnitzel* tasted nothing like her *rántott hús*. "What do you know that they don't?" I'd ask.

More than anything, I'd share stories with Anyu of my adventures in Europe. She didn't mind that I loved living in Germany. She thought it was good for me to experience a new culture. Mostly, she was happy that I was happy. She'd been concerned that I wouldn't be satisfied unless I was in the NBA.

173

By the middle of the season, I'd become a regular in the city center that had captivated me on my first night in Europe. Around town, German women told me they liked my American accent. For my dad, not speaking the language as a foreigner had been debilitating. For me, not speaking the language as a foreigner made me appealing. Yet another example of my privilege.

I finished my lone season in Germany as our team's second-leading scorer. I had 24 points in my second professional game and put up 31 points and seven rebounds in a crucial one-point win near the end of the year. One American teammate had called me "daddy's little girl" during practice and another had threatened to hurt me in the locker room for shooting too much. I never apologized for anything. I stayed focused on proving that I could play at the pro level.

For the first time in my life, though, basketball wasn't the main thing on my mind. I'll never forget telling my dad about her. He'd timed one of his NBA scouting trips to Europe so he could see me play toward the end of my rookie season. He'd met up with my team in the southwest city of Ludwigsburg, a quaint German enclave where the famous Nazi film *Jud Süß* was made at the order of Nazi propaganda minister Joseph Goebbels. Everywhere I played in Germany had a past that had affected my family, but this conversation with my dad would be about the future. He was expecting me to talk about my play when I came out of the locker room after the game, still in my uniform, but I had a different plan. "I need to tell you something," I said as soon as I hugged him hello. "I found someone."

He stared at me. I'd never said anything like that to him before. "Like a girl?" he finally said.

"Yep," I replied, nodding. "Exactly like a girl. And she's the one."

Sam and I had met briefly the summer before I left for Germany and had reconnected through social media during the season.

Everything she said sparkled. I couldn't get enough of her quirky charm. And she was Jewish, too. Our Internet messages to each other became longer and more frequent until phone numbers were exchanged. I'd rush home from practice to call her and would regularly stay up until 8:00 AM talking to her. Before getting to know her, I never would've tired myself out before practice. After getting to know her, I wasn't even thinking about practice.

I'd always been too focused on basketball to establish what I wanted in a partner, but I'm glad I didn't spend time on it. I never could've envisioned Sam. I'd only been in her physical presence for a few hours back in the States, but by the time my season in Germany ended, I already knew I was going to marry her.

Sam changed everything, but even before meeting her, basketball's grip on my life had been loosening. Since my injury, the game's significance had felt fleeting. Its hold over me lacked the severity it had once possessed. I'd lost it all on the court at the moment I tore up my knee, but my life remained the same. My parents were still proud of me. My family still loved me. The world still offered other experiences to enjoy. I started to see basketball as *representing* what mattered most to me instead of *being* what mattered most to me. Success and failure in basketball were temporary. Family and values were forever. The game had always been my vehicle to carry a legacy, but I was learning that there were other ways to carve a meaningful path. Growing apart from basketball basically just meant I was growing up.

When I got home from Germany that summer, I started the process to get my Romanian citizenship. Based on my dad's Romanian heritage, I was eligible for a passport, even though I'd never been to the country before. The irony of the situation was not lost on me. My family had fled Romania, with injustice and anti-Semitism defining their experience, and here I was as an advantaged American trying to regain my family's Romanian status. Professional success for my grandparents had meant getting the hell out of Romania. Somehow, professional success for me meant getting the hell back in.

At the time, basketball leagues in Europe had quotas that limited the number of Americans per team. Romania had joined the European Union in 2007, so having a European passport would be a huge asset on the basketball job market. It took Dad half a year to get the first required document, a copy of his birth certificate from his hometown in Transylvania. He'd given up his citizenship when they left, but this document was proof of my Romanian roots.

I spent that summer in Washington, D.C., where my family had relocated from Milwaukee after my dad had been hired to run Washington's NBA team, and I visited the Romanian Embassy every few weeks to try to manage the passport timeline. It was nearly impossible to get anything done. The Romanians were unperturbed by my urgency. Every new embassy employee I met would greet me in Romanian. "I only speak English," I'd say. I don't think that made them want to help me. By the time my second professional season came around, I was no closer to getting my passport. I barely had any patience left. I couldn't comprehend how my grandparents had stayed sane while waiting a decade to leave Romania.

I played my second professional season as an American in Spain, in the small beachfront city of Gandia, right outside of Valencia. We competed in Spain's second division called LEB Oro. Spain's first division, the ACB, was the best domestic league in the world outside of the NBA. Sam was finishing up her college degree, but she came to live with me for the last month of the season. My apartment was two blocks from the sea, so every morning, we'd wake up to a salty Spanish breeze. We'd eat sweet Valencia oranges before I left for practice and order fresh paella after games. Our favorite restaurant overlooked the Mediterranean. Sam was a Spanish major, which was helpful since my coach didn't speak a word of English. Neither did the majority of my teammates. Whenever someone got cursed out at practice, I'd remember the phrasing so Sam could translate for me. My Spanish was passable but clunky, accented like Dad's English had once been.

In Spain, none of my teammates cared about my family name. No one ever called me "daddy's little girl." I was accepted on the court and in love off of it. Ordinarily, I was sensitive to my surroundings and unable to tune out external noise. Without any noise in Spain other than the crunch of a perfectly crisped paella, I felt light and natural while playing basketball. It wasn't something I was used to. I led our team in scoring and posted the best shooting percentages of my career.

Sam and I were long in love by the time she got to Spain, but she'd never seen me play basketball before. In European leagues, teams that finished at the bottom of the standings were relegated to a lower league the following year. My team was in danger of relegation. We had to win two of our last four games to avoid an embarrassing demotion.

During our hours-long phone conversations when we were falling in love, Sam and I discussed the profound pull that basketball had over my life. She knew about the Holocaust, my uncle, my dad. She could feel the depths of my relationship with the game. In Spain, she watched me play for the first time with a lot riding on the outcome. The four games she attended represent the best sequence of basketball I ever played in my life. It was an out-of-body experience propelled by the exhilaration of young love. It's nice when a friend affirms your choice in a life partner. Basketball had always been one of my best friends, and the verdict on Sam was clear.

The first game she watched, I hit a deep three-pointer to clinch a win and finished with 23 points, one of my highest outputs of the season. I had 21 points one game and 28 points and 10 rebounds another. In a must-win home game, I made six out of seven three-pointers and led my team to victory with 22 points. I was a solid pro player and nothing more. For a few games, Sam helped me know what it felt like to be great. There was something about having Sam at my games that just worked for me. She provided a sense of balance that I'd always needed but could never find.

It was a balance my dad naturally seemed to possess. He didn't yearn for basketball success like I did. He didn't cling to basketball tight enough to squeeze every atom of air out of the ball. He simply showed up every day, thinking less, doing more. He put one foot in front of the other to move away from tragedy, with no awareness that he was climbing a peak toward basketball greatness. I'd had my eyes locked on that summit from the time I was a kid. It was a long, long way up.

chapter 16

king & Queens

T HE U.S. Open was the fourth and final Grand Slam tournament on the pro tennis calendar. The world's best tennis players started the year in the southern hemisphere for the Australian Open, played the clay courts of Roland-Garros for the French Open, donned all white on the grass courts of Wimbledon, and finally ended up in New York City for the U.S. Open, on hard courts, because it was New York City, so of course the courts were hard. Before the U.S. Open moved to what would become Arthur Ashe Stadium in Flushing Meadows, Queens, it was played at the West Side Tennis Club three miles south in Forest Hills. Because of tennis icons like Arthur Ashe, Stan Smith, and Ilie Năstase, the U.S. Open was a tough ticket to get. My dad and his friends didn't need tickets. They knew where the hole in the fence was. They'd glance around before slipping through, entering the stadium undetected. They never paid a penny to watch the best tennis on Earth.

In 1972, Ilie Năstase beat Arthur Ashe in Forest Hills to win the U.S. Open. He was the No. 2 player in the world, and he'd become the first athlete endorsed by Nike. The following year, he earned the world's top ranking. "Where's Năstase from?" one of Dad's friends asked as they lounged in the stands at the U.S. Open and ate sunflower seeds from their pockets. They'd been to the public swimming area at the old World's Fair grounds earlier that day. It was 1969 and Năstase was making his rise toward No. 1. They'd just finished eighth grade. "Romania," Dad answered in perfect English.

He didn't say anything else about it. He was a New Yorker now.

Dad's main link to his European past during his junior high years came each summer when he'd visit his family in Israel. Of Anyu's four siblings who'd survived the War, three of them had settled in the Jewish homeland. Dad would spend weeks with his family in Bnei Brak, Gan Yavne, and Ramat Aviv. His family didn't speak English and he didn't speak Hebrew, so they communicated in Hungarian. He once had an Israeli passport, he reminded them, but that was a long time ago. If not for his brother's love interest who'd moved to the United States, he, too, would have been an Israeli.

Dad floated with his cousins in the Dead Sea and visited the Western Wall in Jerusalem. Israel's streets were dusty and undeveloped. They looked nothing like New York City. Dad spent his free time in search of pickup basketball games. His family thought it was too hot to play ball outside, but where he was from, basketball was life. The game was the best way to belong to something. It was the thread that tied the community together. The weather was irrelevant. It was all about the competition and the camaraderie. The few games Dad found in Israel were different than the games in the city. The hoops were old and rickety, and the kids barely knew the rules. He missed the park.

Over big family dinners on Shabbat, he'd talk about his friends in New York. Many of them were Jewish. In Israel, almost everyone was Jewish. Most parents in Israel had survived the Holocaust. It wasn't just his parents anymore. There was something strangely comforting about that. It was a terrible sense of connection, but a sense of connection, nonetheless.

When school started back in New York, Apu took Dad to Madison Square Garden to watch the Knicks. Apu came straight from work in the Bronx while Dad took the subway from Queens by himself, hopping off the D train at 42nd Street, the site of the old Garden. He felt a rush of energy every time The Garden came into view. He didn't have to be playing basketball for the game to spark joy. Whether spectating or participating, basketball had become his sense of place. He knew that the first thing he'd talk about with his friends the following day would be the Knicks.

Apu and Dad bought the cheapest tickets available and sat high in the rafters, shoulder to shoulder with rabid Knicks fans from across the five boroughs. Dad studied the Knicks players during warmups. He watched their moves, their mannerisms, how they worked. He'd try those things at the park. He observed his surroundings during the game and saw proud New Yorkers all around him flailing their arms and baring their teeth, passionately applauding the good and more passionately berating the bad. In the rafters at the old Garden was where Dad became familiar with the term "jackass." It was directed at Celtics coach Red Auerbach, a Jew from Brooklyn. He also learned the tremendous versatility of the word "fuck," as in "what the fuck is Komives doing?" or "that fucking Riordan has heart" or "Heinsohn, you stupid fuck!" New Yorkers were known for their passion. Basketball was known to bring it out of them.

Under coach Red Holzman, the Knicks had turned into a title contender built on a foundation of toughness and teamwork. They were forceful and physical, a must for a team from New York City, but they also played the game as one. They shared the ball and cooperated. Each player accepted his role and sacrificed for the greater good. Dad was drawn to the leadership and determination of Willis Reed, the flash and finesse of Walt Frazier, the craft and intelligence of Bill Bradley, and the dependability and efficiency of Dick Barnett. His favorite player, by far, was Dave DeBusschere, the Knicks' scrappy and bruising forward from Detroit. DeBusschere wasn't as big and athletic as some at his position, but he'd jump in front of the E train if the Knicks needed it. DeBusschere's big heart thumped through his orange and blue Knicks jersey. Dad liked seeing basketball played with purpose. He liked people who had something to prove. Over the course of a given Knicks game, Dad's eyes would always find their way back to DeBusschere. He tried to model his game after No. 22.

In junior high, Dad's peers caught up to him in size. They suddenly had mustaches and body odor. Those were both new, and only one of them was awesome. Dad didn't have hair under his arms yet, so the upper lip seemed like a pipe dream. Still, despite his lack of development, he was big and strong and able to hold his own at the park. He had a knack for throwing his body around and scoring the basketball. Dad continued to excel in the local CYO league and also played on the team at Russell Sage Junior High School comprised of seventh, eighth, and ninth graders. At first, he was too raw and inexperienced to get in the games. Besides, there were five guys on the team who could dunk, and Dad needed a ladder to touch the rim.

In eighth grade, his Bar Mitzvah service was held at Congregation Ahavath Sholom on 113th Street in Forest Hills. Anyu and Apu saved up to provide pastries and drinks for all temple members who attended the ceremony. Friends of the family were treated to a sit-down lunch afterward consisting of *cholent, challah,* and *blintzes* for dessert.

On weekends when it rained, Dad knew the park would be empty. He'd walk over by himself and shoot hoops for hours. It was the only time he could get his own basket. By his last season of junior high, he'd worked himself into the team's leading scorer. He was 5'10" and earning a reputation in the neighborhood. He'd become better than the other kids, but he didn't think much of it. He didn't know he could play basketball in college. He hadn't grown up thinking he'd even go to college. He'd just watched the Knicks win the NBA Championship in 1970, but he never imagined getting paid to play basketball like Reed or DeBusschere. People like him sat in the nosebleeds at Madison Square Garden. They didn't take the floor to perform for the people.

Every year on April 27, three days after his birthday, he'd visit his brother's grave with his parents. At the cemetery, Anyu's face would be granite, like the tombstone displaying her son's name. Pictures of her from that era are haunting. Her eyes are hollow, her skin sallow and dull. Apu was solemn on those days, maintaining an aura of strength because someone had to. Dad was quiet by the gravesite. His stomach vibrated in a way that only happened when he was near his brother. The hope of basketball had started to part the darkness. Dad played his ball. Anyu and Apu had their work. They spent time as a family and rarely named the obvious absence in their lives.

Dad entered Forest Hills High School in the fall of 1970. He'd walk the same halls as alums such as Simon & Garfunkel, The Ramones, and Spider-Man himself, Peter Parker, who in *Amazing Spider-Man* attends Forest Hills from 1962 to 1965, a few years before Dad enrolled. Dad still couldn't grow a mustache when high school ball started, but sideburns were a possibility. Whether he was speaking Hungarian at home or English in the gym, his voice was hardly recognizable. He was 6'2", his legs and shoulders thick, his butt wide and powerful. He still played at the park, usually in jeans, a T-shirt, and black low-top Converse sneakers, but he didn't worry about losing. The young boy trying to fit in no longer existed. Basketball was the driving force in the neighborhood where he'd once craved acceptance, and Dad was now the best player in that neighborhood.

And it wasn't even close.

One day as Dad controlled the action at the park, he glanced toward the fence and saw his old nemesis Billy walk through. Billy was back from college and had stopped by the park to play ball. Dad's pulse quickened. His eyes focused in. It'd been years since Billy slammed Dad's face into the concrete, over and over and over. Dad had barely known English and was just learning how to play basketball. A lot had changed since then. He was much bigger than Billy now. And he was much, much better at basketball.

Dad led his team to win after win, patiently waiting for Billy to have his turn. When Billy finally got on the court, Dad acknowledged him with a quick head nod before turning to his teammates. "I'll guard him," Dad said, pointing at Billy.

On the first possession of the game, Dad demanded the ball. He bullied Billy down to the block, stuck an elbow into his chest, and hit a turnaround jumper. On the next play, he pushed Billy under the rim, jumped on his back, and cleaned up an offensive rebound. Then he elbowed Billy in the neck as he spun for another bucket. More than anything, he was waiting. Just waiting. He pushed Billy to the block and elbowed him again — this time harder — before laying it in off the glass. Billy finally rushed forward. "What the fuck are you doing?" he yelled as his face burned red.

Decades later, I sat with my dad as he recalled that afternoon at the park. "So you're punishing him," I said, "and he gets in your face. Then what?"

Dad shrugged. "I told him, 'I'm doing the same shit you did to me,'" he said. "Then I did what I'd been waiting to do."

"What's that?"

"I took a few steps toward him and punched him in the face."

I smiled. "And what'd he do?"

My dad's forehead crinkled. "What do you mean?"

"After you hit him," I said. "What'd he do after you hit him?"

He looked away, confused. "What do you mean what'd he do?"

"I mean what'd he do?" I repeated, louder this time. "Did he hit you back?"

Dad looked down at his massive hands. They were like bear paws. His fingers were so thick that my wedding ring could fit inside his wedding ring. My friends used to marvel at his size and girth, regularly asking each other what would happen if Big Ern ever hit one of them in the face. The answer was unanimous: death. The notion of Billy being able to fight back after being punched like that was so ridiculous that it hadn't even crossed Dad's mind. He wasn't trying to be a tough guy. He was just trying to be realistic. "Of course he didn't hit me back," he said. "How could he have hit me back? I hit him. It was over. End of story."

Billy never returned to the park to play ball. Not while Dad ran it, anyway.

Dad averaged 17.4 points and more than 10 rebounds per game as a sophomore at Forest Hills High School, leading the varsity team in scoring and earning All-Queens honors. Games were in the afternoon around 4:00 PM, and since my grandparents' store didn't close until the evening, they hadn't been to a game all season. Neither of them had ever even seen Dad shoot a basketball. In their minds, basketball was just a recreational activity, something that kept their son occupied and out of trouble.

The furthest they went to support this interest was allowing him to scrap the summer visits to Israel. They let him be a waiter with two of his best friends at a camp in the Catskills instead. He served the paying campers breakfast, lunch, and dinner and played basketball the rest of the day. Camp Sequoia offered free room and board and a chance to get out of the city. There was a lake, a baseball field, water skiing, horseback riding, and fresh air in every direction. Dad and his buddies could be found on the courts.

By junior year, he was 6'4" and one of the best basketball players in New York City, averaging more than 20 points and 15 rebounds per game. Every night, Anyu made him *ciorba, húsleves, libamáj, rántott hús*. He never stopped eating and never stopped growing. He played the game hard, always hard, like he'd learned at the park.

He competed with an edge, like you'd expect from someone who'd been ostracized for not being able to speak English.

Despite his success, his parents had still never seen a game. What were they going to do? Close the store early? One winter day, the phone at the store rang. It was Dad's high school coach, Queens coaching legend Irwin Isser. "Mrs. Grunfeld," Coach Isser said as Anyu answered, "you need to come watch your son play basketball. He's the captain of our team and the most determined player I've ever coached. He'll be able to go to college for this. He's gifted."

Anyu hung up the phone. *Her son, gifted?* A few nights after the call, my grandparents approached Forest Hills High School. Since they'd kept the store open as late as possible before heading to the gym, they arrived after the game had started. The usher at the door barely looked at them as he shared the news. "Gym's full," the usher told my grandparents when they tried to enter.

They could hear the ball bouncing. Anyu signaled to Apu. He'd never really learned the language. "We come guests of coach," he said. "Parents of player."

The usher shook his head. "Nothing I can do," he said. "No room left."

Anyu steadied her gaze. "Ernie Grunfeld is our son's name," she chimed in, making every attempt to straighten her crooked English.

The usher's eyes expanded as he grabbed the door handle. "Why didn't you say so?"

The doors swung open, and Anyu and Apu moved into the packed gymnasium. It was cold and windy outside but hot and sticky in the gym. The game was in progress. Standing near the wall, Apu scanned the court for Dad, without luck. Fans were stomping their feet and cheering. Apu yelled over the noise to Anyu in Hungarian. "If he's so good," he said, "then why isn't he playing?"

Anyu did a double take and pointed to the middle of the floor. "*Shunyi*," she said, using my grandpa's Hungarian name. "Look right there. That's Ernie."

Jézus Krisztus, my grandpa thought.

He was used to seeing my dad in sweats and a T-shirt or maybe jeans and a sweatshirt, but there he stood in a basketball uniform for the first time. He suddenly looked more like a man than a boy, with his big frame stretching his jersey's fabric to its limits, his arms flexed and legs fired, his wide shoulders bearing down on his opponents, his huge hands hanging easily by his sides. My grandparents' youngest son — a displaced refugee trying to outrun tragedy — had found a place where he spoke the language better than anyone. The balance of power had shifted, for once, in their direction.

His hidden stature somehow held the promise of a bigger future than my grandparents had imagined. Anyu grabbed Apu's hand and squeezed. Apu had been a great sportsman in his day, though his options were limited by the Holocaust and communism. In America, there didn't seem to be any limits to what was possible. Anyu's eyes were already filled with tears. After the game, a win against Bronx High School of Science, Apu told Dad he'd be at the next one. He also said that Dad never had to come work at the store again. He should focus on his basketball. They'd take care of the rest.

Apu was in attendance for Dad's first playoff game that year as he faced off against Rudy Jackson from John Bowne High School in Flushing, Queens. Jackson, one of New York's top players, would star at Wichita State before being drafted by the Knicks. The namesake of Dad's opponent for the playoff opener, John Bowne, was a 17th century English immigrant to what would become the British colony of New York. John Bowne is known as a pioneer for religious liberty, having influenced the progressive religious thinking of the framers of the U.S. Constitution. Given Dad's family history with both religion and liberty, he should've treated a school named after John Bowne with some respect. Instead, he made 17-of-18 field goals and finished the victory with 41 points. A Jewish immigrant's gotta do what a Jewish immigrant's gotta do.

It was basketball that had been there for my dad when his life came crashing down. Now, it was time to fly.

The *New York Post* named him second-team All-City that year. The following season, his senior year, he averaged 25 points and 18 rebounds. Apu rarely missed a home game. They'd been in the country less than a decade, but Dad was now an All-American. He was also one of the most highly recruited players in the country. More than 150 colleges sent letters to the high school. Dad hadn't grown up with the university system and hadn't known anyone in Romania who'd gone to college. Now he had some of the most prominent schools in the world begging him to attend. He wasn't sure what it all meant, and he couldn't rely on his parents for help. He sought guidance from his friend and mentor, Tom Konchalski, a beloved New York talent scout who would become the greatest evaluator of high school basketball players in history. Dad was one of the first New York kids he discovered.

It didn't take long for the college coaches to start descending. St. John's, Fordham, and Rutgers were local, so they'd come to the school, to the apartment, and to the store. Dick Vitale at Rutgers sent a handwritten note every day. They always featured many exclamation points. Chuck Daly wrote from Penn, Lefty Driesell visited from Maryland, and Digger Phelps flew in from Notre Dame. Al McGuire from Marquette made the trip and took Dad to lunch at Pastrami King on Queens Boulevard. Michigan, Virginia, Syracuse, and Kentucky were all regulars.

Dad did most of the talking, since Anyu and Apu still struggled with the language. They mostly listened, even when the Kentucky coaches showed up at the apartment on Sunday mornings unannounced. Anyu would be vacuuming, and Dad would be at the park. "Just passing through the neighborhood," they'd say, as if Lexington, Kentucky bordered Queens, New York.

The Kentucky staff once took Dad to Belmont Park, the famous racetrack in New York that hosts the Belmont Stakes, the final leg of horse racing's Triple Crown. At Belmont, Kentucky arranged for Dad to tour the grounds and meet some of the horses. He walked by the sandy stables and admired the beasts. He observed huge heads and gentle eyes. One horse in particular stood out. It was massive and powerful. Its coat was a beautiful brown color, so deep and rich that it was almost red. There was a white streak starting above the eyes and trickling down to the mid-nose. Dad stood next to the specimen and patted its muscular hindquarters. A Kentucky coach snapped a photo of the two athletes. People said Dad was as big as a horse, but he sure as hell wasn't as big as this horse.

The year the photo was taken, 1973, the horse would set a world record at the Belmont Stakes, winning by 31 lengths, the largest margin in the 105-year history of the race. Having already won the Kentucky Derby and the Preakness, Dad's new friend, Secretariat, completed the Triple Crown. When he passed away years later, Secretariat proved the power of heart in sports. His was estimated to weigh 22 pounds. The average thoroughbred's heart weighed 8.5.

Dad enjoyed the races, but Anyu didn't approve. She thought bringing him to a racetrack promoted gambling and debauchery. Where he went to college was his decision, but she made her stance clear: she in no way wanted him to spend four years with those scoundrels from the University of Kentucky.

Not far from Lexington was the University of Tennessee, in Knoxville. No school was more committed to getting Dad to play basketball for them than the Tennessee Volunteers. Their lead assistant, Stu Aberdeen, a close friend of Dad's mentor, Tom Konchalski, stood by the doors of Dad's high school every day for a month, waiting for the bell to ring. He'd be wearing a bright orange blazer, the famous color of the Vols. He followed Dad home each day, trying to convince him to come down to Knoxville. Eventually, Dad started avoiding the coach by using the back door when school ended. During the day, Aberdeen would visit the store and loiter around the cash register as Anyu and Apu worked. "Give him orange juice in the morning," he'd tell Anyu and Apu, "and an orange pencil to write with, and orange socks to sleep in."

Dad took official recruiting visits to Tennessee, Kentucky, Virginia, Notre Dame, Michigan, Syracuse, Fordham, and Penn. At Notre Dame, head football coach Ara Parseghian took one look at Dad and told him he should come play football for the Irish, too. With my dad checking in at 6'5", 220 pounds, Parseghian thought he'd make a great tight end. Dad knew more about European football than American football, so he just smiled and nodded.

After skipping his high school graduation to play in the finals of a basketball tournament, Dad narrowed his college choices to Tennessee and Syracuse. Weeks later, he committed to play basketball for the University of Tennessee. He thought he could play right away as a freshman at Tennessee, in the best conference in the country, the SEC. And Knoxville was close enough to New York for his parents to visit, so Anyu was happy, especially since she'd be traveling to Tennessee and not Kentucky.

Tennessee was down south, where there was widespread anti-Semitism, but Dad had felt comfortable when he visited. No one said anything about his beliefs or his background. They treated him like a king. That was before he knew he'd be joined at the University of Tennessee by a real King. Together, they'd form one of the greatest duos in college basketball history.

chapter 17

ring & run

I DIDN'T THINK MUCH ABOUT BEING INVITED TO A FREE-agent minicamp with the New York Knicks. Minicamps during the summer let NBA teams evaluate prospects over a couple days of scrimmages, and I'd been approached by a few franchises based on my successful first season in Spain. A bone spur in my ankle kept me from pursuing all but one of these NBA opportunities. The timing happened to work for me to attend camp with the team my dad had been with for 17 seasons. It was the same team my grandpa and dad had watched from the cheap seats in Madison Square Garden and the same team that'd played in the first NBA basketball game shortly after my grandparents survived the Holocaust. It was the same team I'd grown up worshipping.

There was no nostalgia when I got to the Knicks practice facility for the three-day event. I was a grown man now, and this was business. There were 19 players invited in total. Some were from top leagues in Europe while others already had careers in the NBA. The goal for all players at this minicamp was to earn an invite to training camp with the Knicks in the fall. Only one or two players — if any — would get that invite. I'd done well the previous season, but I hadn't played at the highest level in Europe. My career to that point was one of the least impressive of all the guys at the tryout.

When I walked into the locker room, I saw a whiteboard listing the three teams for the scrimmages. There were two teams of six and one team of seven. For the team of seven, my name was the final one listed, as if I were the last guy selected. I had my own row on the board that might as well have been labeled: "In case of an emergency, play this asshole." I'm sure no one else was paying much attention, but my dad had been a longtime player for the Knicks. He used to be the president and general manager of the team. Having my name on its own line made me feel like I'd been invited as a favor. And maybe I had been. Either way, that nepotism nerve was always raw for me, so the anger that surfaced didn't have to travel far.

Luckily, I caught a few breaks at the minicamp. First, the Knicks had just hired a new coach, Mike D'Antoni, and the assistant coaches installed his pass-and-move offense. I was a pass-and-move player myself, unable to create my own shot but effective when I worked with my teammates to find advantages. The offense fit my game perfectly. The second break I caught was that someone on my team had a minor injury that kept him out of camp. That meant more playing time for me. I was still training with Frank during the summers, so I was in the best shape of anyone there. More minutes were welcome. The third and most important break I caught was that I'd been listed as the extra guy on the team with the extra guy. My dad always said I played better when I was mad.

I scored 26 points the first game and surpassed 20 in the other two games, too. Some basketball players produce symphonies, with every note building off the last until a beautifully nuanced rhythm is created. That wasn't me. I was a hyperactive teenager banging a drum in his garage. I had no artistry but a great deal of enthusiasm. I'd hit a few jumpers, sneak away with a back cut, find the lane for my floater, clean up on the glass, get out in transition, do whatever the hell I could to get an easy bucket. It wasn't pretty, but the points added up. I finished as one of the camp's top scorers. *Last on the list, my ass,* was how I thought about it.

My dad ran into Knicks general manager Donnie Walsh a few weeks later. Donnie said I'd been the best player at the tryout. He invited me to training camp with the Knicks not long after. I was still waiting on my Romanian passport, so the timing was perfect.

The passport was close, but I wanted to hold off on signing overseas until I had it. I accepted the Knicks' invite and would be part of the team on a non-guaranteed NBA contract. Faces of Knicks players used to stare down at me from my bedroom ceiling. Now, I'd be a Knicks player — even if my future with the team was uncertain.

It's too bad I wasn't able to celebrate the achievement. I was already telling myself that no one would take me seriously. I didn't have enough perspective to realize that people were far too busy with their own lives to spend their time thinking about me. I was just wasting my time thinking about them. That time would have been much better spent appreciating how special it was, how much damn history there was, every time I slipped my own Knicks jersey over my shoulders.

The Knicks already had the league maximum 15 players under contract, so to make the team I'd need someone to get cut, traded, or bought out. Still, I planned on making the team. I'd scored 45 when I needed it in high school and was the most improved player in the country when I needed it in college. I'd seen a journey from the Holocaust to the NBA, so I was unphased by long odds. I signed my deal and hoped for one more break.

Knicks training camp was held in upstate New York. Days before we took the 20-minute flight on our team plane, a Knicks staffer presented me with a No. 18 practice jersey with my name on it. I was used to seeing that model of Knicks jersey in an older vintage. The team assumed I'd wear the number my dad had worn, but I couldn't do it. I told them I'd be wearing No. 9 instead. The No. 18 orange and blue was sacred in my house. My dad was the only Jewish player ever to wear Judaism's most symbolic number for the Knicks. No Jew had even played for the Knicks since him. If I made the team and could represent New York and its Jews as a real NBA player, I'd consider No. 18. As a camp invite who hadn't accomplished anything, I opted for half of that. As soon as I got my No. 9 Knicks jersey with my name on the back, I mailed Anyu a picture of me wearing it. She put the picture on her refrigerator, where I like to think it stood guard over the *rántott hús*.

When we arrived at the hotel in Saratoga, New York for training camp, I hustled to my room to take a nap. I was a bundle of nerves, and I needed to get ready for the evening session. Not long after I fell asleep, the hotel phone rang, interrupting my preparation. Frustrated, I rolled over and grabbed the phone off the receiver. It was David Lee, the Knicks' starting power forward who'd become a friend during my time with the team. "Hey," I said.

"Hey," he said.

"What's up?" I asked.

"We don't have poker chips," he said.

"Me neither," I said.

"We're going to play poker all week and need chips. The guys want you to run and get some."

My bed was so comfortable. I could feel my nap dying a painful death. *Welcome to the NBA, I suppose.* "All right," I said. "I'll take care of it."

I hung up the phone with no idea where to get poker chips in Saratoga, New York. I threw on my Knicks sweats and had the front desk call me a cab. I told the driver to take me to the nearest Costco. After a 10-minute ride, I was relieved when I found a lonely set of poker chips sitting on a random shelf in a random aisle in this random Costco. I snatched up the chips and bought them with my hard-earned European hoops money. On the way back to the hotel, I felt a strange sense of accomplishment. I'd solved a problem for my NBA teammates. I'd come through. I'd done enough to earn some respect from the guys. I needed every ounce I could get.

I hurried to the poker room to deliver the chips to my teammates. In my heart, I want to believe that someone said thank you when I handed the chips over and the door closed in my face. I'm not sure I heard those words. I *am* sure that no one mentioned my good deed again, nor did anyone reimburse me for the cab rides or the poker chips. After a week of training camp, I asked one of my teammates how poker was going. He was an NBA veteran who'd made tens of millions of dollars in his career. He told me he was up $56,000 for the week. I didn't have the guts to ask for my 60 bucks back. Lord knows I wanted to.

Despite a stronger training camp than anyone expected, I only saw minutes in one of our preseason games, grabbing a single rebound and missing the two free throws I attempted. I had to call my mom from the bus after the game so she could calm me down about missing those free throws.

We played several of our preseason games at Madison Square Garden. Its smells and sounds were familiar, but I felt a distance. Walking through the bowels of The Garden was like visiting a childhood home that now belonged to a new family. Part of me was at ease in The Garden. Another part of me was a foreigner. I'd stored away the pain I'd felt after my dad was fired by the Knicks, but it still existed somewhere deep. The Garden could never feel the same as it did back then. Life had moved on, but there was still something inside me that hadn't.

Sam drove down from grad school to watch me take the floor at The Garden as a member of the Knicks. I ended up not getting in the game, so all she had to show for her trip was a finger callus from snapping photos of me sitting on the bench. In practices between games, I scored more than I should have, dove for loose balls, and threw my body around like my dad had for the Knicks. I ended up making it to the last game of the preseason before getting cut.

One of our assistant coaches told me that Coach D'Antoni wanted to talk to me after a game. I knew what that meant. He said I'd done a good job, but they had to let me go. I thanked him for the opportunity. I walked out of Coach D'Antoni's office at The Garden and took advantage of the flu shots they were giving out in the locker room. I'd been cut from my beloved Knicks a few minutes earlier, so the least I could do was save myself a trip to Walgreens. I exited The Garden that night out of the same door I used to follow my dad through after playoff games during the '90s. I was uncharacteristically content. I'd proven that I could hang in the NBA, but I also had accepted that the NBA was a stretch for me.

I was a good basketball player, but I wasn't great. I didn't have whatever my dad had. I couldn't just play my game and make it in the NBA. I needed luck, circumstance, and a coach who truly believed in me, but I didn't have much energy left to seek them out. My window was too small. Once I had my Romanian passport, the opportunity cost would be too big. I knew I'd never give the NBA another shot. Europe was my family's past, but it had become my future. My path would be different than I'd always imagined, and I'd come to terms with that. Sam and I would make the journey together.

A few months after being cut by the Knicks, my Romanian citizenship was approved. Romania's basketball federation had helped with my passport with the understanding that I'd play for their national team the following summer. Even with the federation's help, it'd taken a year and a half to get it done. I went to a ceremony at the embassy in Washington, D.C. and received documentation confirming my status. I wore ill-fitting khakis and an old blazer as I held a Romanian flag and read an oath in Romanian. I tried to sound out the words but had no idea what the hell I was saying.

It was hard to focus with my sister sitting in the first row taking pictures and laughing at me. She wasn't making fun of me for not speaking the language properly. We don't do that in our family. We do, however, make fun of absurd situations. I'd never been to Romania, but now I was a Romanian. She couldn't help but laugh. It'd been 40 years since our dad had fled the country — unaware of the black-market money *his* dad had hidden under a seat in the front of the train. He no longer spoke Romanian, only Hungarian. Anyu spoke both. Now that I had my citizenship, Anyu asked if I'd visit Micula one day. She wondered aloud what was left of it.

I stopped in Bucharest to pick up my passport then headed back to Spain for another season. I'd again signed in the Spanish second division, this time with Club Baloncesto Valladolid, a team that'd dropped down from the first division the year before. The club in Valladolid had a rich basketball history, having been home to Hall of Famers Arvydas Sabonis and Oscar Schmidt. The team was adding me midseason to help them win the league title and earn promotion back to the best league in Europe, the ACB. If we could win it all, I'd be guaranteed a contract in the ACB for the following season, making more than $20,000 a month after taxes.

With Sam finishing grad school in the United States, I lived by myself my whole second year in Spain. The team gave me a four-story townhouse in a new development in the suburbs. Without Sam, I was immediately lonely. Being isolated in a big house didn't help. On my first night, I carried the mattress from my upstairs bedroom to my downstairs living room. I placed it on the floor next to the window, and that's where I slept for the entire season. I was a solid contributor and starter on my team, but I was far from a star. My biggest individual accomplishment that year, by far, was turning a four-story townhouse into a studio apartment.

My team was atop the standings for the majority of the year, and Dad was scouting in Madrid the week we had a chance to clinch the title at the end of the season. He took the train to Valladolid to catch the deciding game. When the buzzer sounded and we became champions, I picked my dad out of the crowd. That wasn't a hard thing to do, since he was twice the size of everyone else and had a mustache that could basically shout my name. "Best league in Europe next year!" he yelled when I gave him a bear hug, my jersey still soaked with sweat.

I partied with my teammates in Spain for a week to celebrate the championship. I even took a shot of vodka to commemorate the occasion. It was one of the only alcoholic drinks I'd ever had in my life. It was absolutely horrible. Throughout the week, we visited the mayor's office, did press junkets, and had five-course Spanish dinners that lasted into the morning. One night we rode a float through the city in an elaborate victory parade. It was dusk, and the breeze was hot. The stone sidewalks held centuries of Spain's secrets, from Ferdinand and Isabella to the Spanish Inquisition to Franco to freedom. Valladolid had been founded in 1071. It'd seen it all. I took videos of our fans lining the streets and chanting for our team. I waved as the float rolled past.

As the amber sun faded, our victory float glided into our city's Plaza Mayor. Thousands of our supporters were waiting for us in the square. They waved banners, scarves, and flags. They sang songs. Our team was escorted to the top of the plaza's tallest building. We overlooked the packed space. We'd made this city proud. One by one, my teammates were handed a microphone to address the crowd in Spanish. My Spanish was adequate but nothing more. I'd never given a victory speech in a foreign language — let alone to a sea of impassioned Spaniards. When I was handed the mic, I felt the familiar fear of being limited by language. I stepped forward and looked down on our fans. A wall of faces stared up at me. I already had my entire speech planned out. I knew it wouldn't take long. "¡Dos palabras!" I screamed into the microphone, raising two fingers high in the air and pausing a beat to let my words reverberate across the square. "*¡SOMOS CAMPEONES!*"

I extended my fist above my head. The crowd erupted. It took little effort to translate my speech into English. "Two words," I'd said. "We're champions!"

I handed the mic to the next guy as my teammates patted my shoulders and laughed. I wasn't in the NBA, but I was a champion, and it felt like I was living my childhood dream.

Before flying back to the States, I made sure to pay one last visit to my favorite Spanish restaurant in town. I sat alone with a smile and enjoyed my *pollo a la plancha, patatas bravas,* and *pan con tomate.* It was a delicious Spanish meal, but if I'm being honest, it wasn't in the same league as Anyu's stuff.

chapter 18

mettle & gold

THE RADIO WAS ON AT THE STORE. THE SPORTS segment aired every half hour. Anyu turned it up. She and Apu huddled around, hoping the news would come. They knew an important announcement involving their son would be made soon, but they didn't know when. Anyu hadn't touched her breakfast that morning. She tried and failed to slow her pulse.

To pass time, she flipped through one of the many copies of *Sports Illustrated* that still littered the store. Friends had sent the magazine with a note attached. Amazed customers had dropped off an issue when they shopped, hardly able to believe that the boy was so big and that his English was so good. Anyu had bought dozens from newsstands across the city, just to have them. She'd routinely walk a half mile out of her way to get horseradish for 10 cents less than at the store around the corner, but purchasing this magazine was exempt from all normal measures of prudence and frugality. Her face glowed as she handed over her money.

The *Sports Illustrated* magazines were a few months old now, dated February 9, 1976. On the cover was a picture of a thick white guy with long hair and a slender Black guy with a wide smile. They were both wearing orange and white Tennessee Volunteer basketball uniforms. The text above the picture said, "Double Trouble from Tennessee." Bernard King was from Fort Greene, Brooklyn. Dad was from Queens. They were known as the "Ernie and Bernie Show." Tennessee fans idolized them. SEC opponents hated their brash style, straight from the streets of New York. Bernard wore No. 53. Dad wore No. 22 after his Knicks hero, Dave DeBusschere. The poor Black guy from the Brooklyn projects and the working-class white immigrant from Queens made a fine pair. One battled the dark cloud of poverty. The other lived under a shadow of tragedy. The game of basketball served as their armor.

Sports Illustrated described the "Ernie and Bernie" phenomenon well: "King teases opponents with his lightning-fast, in-your-face jumper. Grunfeld repeatedly bangs them over the head with his bruising drives. King leads the league in scoring (26.8 points per game), while Grunfeld is second with 24.3. Both are among the nation's top 10 scorers — King is seventh, Grunfeld ninth — and if they stay that way it will be only the second time a team has had two in that category. Coaches usually pontificate about the value of balanced scoring, but, understandably, not Tennessee Coach Ray Mears, who admits, 'We have a star system.' His unorthodox strategy has led the Vols to some celestial heights — they have a 14-2 overall record and a No. 9 national ranking."

At the time of the *Sports Illustrated* cover story, Bernard was a sophomore at Tennessee and my dad was a junior. Bernard had been named SEC Player of the Year as a freshman, and he'd win it again as a sophomore. Dad had been named All-SEC first team as a freshman and sophomore, and he'd earn the honor again as a junior. He and Bernard would average more than 50 points combined that season — Dad at 25.3 points per game, Bernard at 25.2.

After each road game the Vols played, the Tennessee team manager had a crucial job to complete. He'd run up the arena's stairs when the horn sounded, entering the opposing team's concourse in his bright orange blazer and locating the nearest pay phone. As Kentucky Wildcat fans cursed him in Rupp Arena or Florida Gator faithful taunted him in Alligator Alley, he made a collect call to a number he could repeat in his sleep: 212-268-4480. When Apu answered in the apartment after one ring, the manager told him how the team had done and how many points my dad had scored. My grandparents couldn't go to sleep until they knew how he'd played. Luckily, the news from the manager was almost always good.

My dad had modeled his game after the blue-collar Dave DeBusschere, developing a playing style that was physical and punishing. He'd conditioned himself as a kid to block things out, so nothing could distract him on the court. Being treated as an illiterate immigrant in America had only fueled his competitive drive, and once he grew big, strong, and fluent, he unleashed that pain on his opponents. His massive legs and butt allowed him to carve out space whenever and wherever he wanted, but it was his work ethic that amplified his ability. Dad grew up watching Anyu and Apu work seven-day weeks in the store. They had nothing when they came to America. They couldn't speak the language and had no formal education. They lost a son. Despite it all, they built a good life in their new country through work. "If you work hard," Apu would always say, "good things will happen."

The notion was simple. Don't sit in a room and plan your success. Don't obsess over where the road may take you. There is too much unpredictability in life to waste energy trying to understand every component of a situation. Boil it down to what's within your control: work. Put the time in and go to bed satisfied. From *Sports Illustrated*: "Grunfeld, the only member of the Vols who is allowed to think 'me first, King second,' is just as effective. Pro scouts rate him equal — or perhaps superior — to King, because he is so rugged. His father insists that Grunfeld not take a summer job so that he can work on refining his basketball skills. The son repays his dad with diligence. Grunfeld was a 58% free-throw shooter in high school. As a Tennessee freshman he made 73% and last year he hit 81% after wearing out countless nets while practicing."

The thought of being a better pro prospect than Bernard King, now an all-time great and an NBA Hall of Famer, has always made my dad chuckle. Nonetheless, his talent opened amazing and unlikely doors for someone born under communism in Romania. The most profound opportunity was to represent his adopted homeland, the United States of America, in international play. It started the summer after high school. Before heading to Knoxville, he competed for Team USA in the Maccabiah Games, the Jewish Olympics, in Israel. He won a silver medal for the United States, losing in the gold medal game to the Israelis, led by Jewish basketball legends Tal Brody and Mickey Berkowitz. Israel's basketball was slowly improving. Dad was the youngest guy on the U.S. team but its leading scorer. Anyu and Apu made the trip to Israel to visit family and watch the games. Dad got flowers for being high scorer and gave them to Anyu in the stands.

A few years later, after his sophomore season at Tennessee, Dad was invited by USA Basketball to play for America's national team for the first time. He'd compete in the International Cup in Yugoslavia, Czechoslovakia, Italy, and Russia on a team coached by Dave Gavitt of Providence. A problem soon emerged, though: Dad wasn't really an American. As the team prepared to leave training camp in Rhode Island to make the flight overseas, they were told to bring their passports to practice. All Dad had was a green card. He told the coaches and USA Basketball administrators that he didn't have a passport. They were stunned. It was an international competition. Dad had traveled overseas before with his green card, but to compete for USA Basketball, he needed to be a citizen with a passport.

In high school, he'd gotten lucky with a good draft number during the Vietnam War and never got called to duty. He would have been able to fight and die for America with only a green card but representing the country in basketball required a passport. "You're from New York City, right?" Dad's perplexed coaches asked. "From Queens?"

Dad shrugged. "Not originally," he said with what by now was a heavy New York accent.

After some research, USA Basketball determined that he was eligible for a passport since he'd been in America for more than 10 years. Everyone exhaled. The USA Basketball staff arranged it all. He missed a practice in Providence and flew to Washington, D.C. for the day.

Someone from USA Basketball met him at the airport. All his forms had already been filled out. Dad returned to Providence the next day with his passport in hand. It had taken his parents 10 years to get their documents to leave Romania. Now, because of Dad's scoring ability, American citizenship was a 24-hour endeavor.

Later that summer, he made the U.S. Pan American team that won gold in Mexico City. Washington's Marv Harshman was the coach. Jud Heathcote, who'd coach Magic Johnson at Michigan State, was the assistant. The team went undefeated. Dad was its second-leading scorer, trailing only Otis Birdsong from the University of Houston. Robert Parish, future Boston Celtics legend and NBA Hall of Famer, was the team's third-leading scorer.

A solid track record representing the U.S. across the ocean meant little once Olympic trials came around. Being an Olympian was an eternal designation. There was nothing more prestigious or competitive than the Olympic Games. This was before the U.S. allowed professionals to compete, so every college player in the country wanted to perform on the biggest international stage in Montreal, wearing the red, white, and blue. At the previous Olympics in Munich in 1972, the U.S. men's basketball team had lost the gold medal in the last seconds when referees allowed the Soviets to redo their final play. It was one of basketball's greatest controversies. That U.S. team led by Doug Collins never accepted the silver medal. It was the first time the U.S. hadn't won gold in basketball since it became an Olympic sport in 1936, in Berlin, in the heart of Nazi Germany.

The 1976 Olympics in Montreal were a chance at redemption. USA Basketball had chosen a coach with a prominence matching the occasion: North Carolina's Dean Smith. He was assisted by Bill Guthridge from his staff at UNC, as well as Georgetown's head coach John Thompson. Sixty of the nation's top players were invited to the tryouts in Raleigh, at North Carolina State University. Only 12 would make the team.

Weeks before tryouts, the coaches sent a notice saying there'd be a timed mile run at the beginning of the trial. Depending on his position, each player had to meet a certain threshold. If not, he'd have to run the mile every day before practice until he hit his mark. Dad was a wing, meaning he had to run it in under 5:45. He was 6'6", 225 pounds and not known for his speed. The only greyhound he'd ever been compared to had wheels and a toilet in the back. He was on the track every day leading up to tryouts. Since he didn't own running shoes, he ran in his Converse basketball sneakers, often with a rubber suit on to lose weight.

As Dad's top conditioning helped him sprint down the home stretch during the mile race at the Olympic trials, he saw a short and stocky white guy at the finish line holding a stopwatch. It was Boston Celtics coach Red Auerbach, the man who would eventually become Celtics general manager and draft Larry Bird. He was there scouting. He wanted to see who had the guts to push through the finish line. Dad clocked in at 5:31, the eighth fastest time at the tryout.

He'd only called home a few times from the trials in Raleigh. Anyu knew he'd done great on the mile and was playing well, but there was competition everywhere. Quinn Buckner and Scott May had just posted an undefeated season at Indiana under Bobby Knight. Walter Davis, Phil Ford, Mitch Kupchak, and Tom LaGarde were all standouts on Dean Smith's team at North Carolina. Steve Sheppard, Dad's high school rival from DeWitt Clinton in the Bronx, was now a star at Maryland. There was Adrian Dantley from Notre Dame, Phil Hubbard from Michigan, Kenny Carr from NC State. And, of course, the one and only Bernard King from Tennessee. The list of talent went on.

When the clock again struck the hour, the sports reporter's voice crackled through Tremont Fabrics. Anyu and Apu ran to the radio and hovered over it. "And now a special announcement," the voice said. "We've been handed the roster for the 1976 U.S. Men's Olympic Basketball Team that will go for gold in Montreal..."

Anyu squeezed Apu's hand. She'd dreamt of this moment ever since Dad got the invite. For her son to be an Olympian for the United States of America after the Holocaust, communism, and the death of his brother was unimaginable. It didn't seem like the universe could finally be this giving. "Ladies and gentlemen," the announcer said, "your 1976 U.S. Men's Olympic Basketball Team: Walter Davis from the University of North Carolina, Phil Ford from the University of North Carolina, Mitch Kupchak from the University of North Carolina, Tom LaGarde from the University of North Carolina..."

Anyu knew the coach was from the University of North Carolina, but that was the only school she was hearing. "Tate Armstrong from Duke University." Her heart pounded. "Phil Hubbard from the University of Michigan, Adrian Dantley from the University of Notre Dame..."

Anyu glanced at Apu. Both of their faces were frozen. The names were coming so fast that it was hard to keep count. Anyu lost track of how many spots were left, but it didn't matter. "Ernie Grunfeld from the University of Tennessee."

Anyu screamed and jumped into Apu's arms. She began to weep. When she looked up at my grandpa, he too was wiping away tears. After taking a minute to regain her composure, Anyu ran next door to see her friends at the neighboring clothing shop. "My son made the Olympic team!" she yelled as soon as she entered.

Anyu wasn't much of a yeller. Her surprised friend popped out from behind the counter and gave her a hug. "Congratulations!" she said. "What country?"

Anyu smiled. Who could blame the friend? They were immigrants who spoke jumbled English. It was a reasonable question to ask. Anyu tapped her chest, right above the heart. "The United States of America," she said.

When Anyu and Apu got home that night, the first thing they did was make their arrangements to attend the Olympics. They'd drive from New York to Montreal and close the store for two whole weeks. It was an unthinkable amount of time not to work, but it was an easy decision. Their best friends Joe and Helen would join them in Montreal. They'd known Dad since he was a kid in Romania. Joe had been a cook in the labor camp with Apu. Helen had survived Auschwitz.

Dad was the only SEC player who made the Olympic team. To his amazement, Bernard King had been cut. Dad thought Bernard was one of the best players on the court. It was a mystery why he was left off the team. Bernard wasn't the only great player not to make the roster. Jack Sikma would become a seven-time All-Star and an NBA Hall of Famer. Otis Birdsong was a four-time All-Star and a second-team All-NBA selection. Cedric Maxwell was Finals MVP for the Celtics in 1981 and has his No. 31 jersey hanging in the rafters in Boston next to Larry Bird's No. 33. Tree Rollins from Wake

Forest led the NBA in blocks in 1983. Michigan's Rickey Greene was an All-Star for Utah in 1984. All these great players were cut from the Olympic team.

Training camp for the Olympics was held in Chapel Hill, North Carolina. On day one, the team went around the room so each player could introduce himself. Coach Smith then asked the team manager to stand up and do the same. A manager was usually relegated to the background — useful merely for cleaning the laundry and delivering cups of water — but not on this team. "You'll show him the same respect you show one another," Coach Smith said. "We're all in this together." Dean Smith was a man of honor. Any Jewish mother would've called him a *mensch*. He was already training his players to think team first, me second.

Leading up to Montreal, Dad traveled the country with Team USA to scrimmage a variety of opponents, including the Denver Nuggets of the American Basketball Association, the Allentown Jets of the Eastern Basketball Association, and the Spanish national team. Anyu and Apu drove from New York to Washington, D.C. for an exhibition game against a fitting opponent: the Israeli national team. Anyu became emotional before the game when Simcha Dinitz, Israeli Ambassador to the United States, was announced to the crowd and referred to as "his excellency." She was used to hearing Jews being called "pigs" and "devils."

In Washington, D.C., Dad stayed with his Olympic teammates at the Watergate Hotel, the site of president Richard Nixon's scandal a few years prior. Watergate ended Nixon's presidency and destroyed his legacy. Less publicized were the taped recordings from that era in which Nixon, while president of the United States of America, lamented that Washington was "full of Jews" before stating his opinions that "most Jews are disloyal" and "the Jews are born spies" and "generally speaking, you can't trust the bastards." Anyu knew that the public reverence for his excellency Simcha Dinitz had a private dark side. She just wasn't aware that it existed in the highest office of the land.

After beating the Israelis, Team USA continued its preparation for Montreal. Before one of the next exhibition games, several of Dad's teammates were one minute late to the pregame meal. The late arrivals hurried to the first open seats they could find, which happened to be at Dad's table. Phil Ford sank down in a seat next to Dad. "Damn," he said. "We're late."

"It's only a minute," Dad said, nudging his teammate's elbow. "Don't worry about it."

"You don't know Coach Smith," he said.

Phil Ford played for Dean Smith at North Carolina. A few minutes after the group had sat, Coach Smith came over to the table. "You all were a minute late," he said in a steady voice. He paused for a second then walked away. That was all that was said on the topic. None of them played the first half of the scrimmage. Three of them were starters and integral to the team's success, but it didn't matter. Dean Smith's leadership style was based on discipline, respect, and accountability. They'd do things the right way on and off the court or they wouldn't do anything at all.

By the time they arrived in Montreal for the Games of the XXI Olympiad, Dad and his teammates were already a cohesive unit. They moved into the dorms in the Olympic Village and slept on bunk beds in a one-bedroom apartment. There were four beds in the bedroom and eight in the living room. They all shared one bathroom. Dad scored a bottom bunk. There were always athletes moving around the village, in the cafeteria, in the hallways, and on the outside pathways. They played dozens of sports and represented even more countries. When Dad wasn't practicing or napping, he and his teammates would grab their Olympic credentials and watch swimming, track and field, volleyball, boxing, or gymnastics.

The U.S. track and field and boxing teams were on the same floor in the dorm, so Dad tried to catch the fights of the boxers he walked past every day, guys like Sugar Ray Leonard, Leon Spinks, Michael Spinks, and Big John Tate. He also kept tabs on Bruce Jenner, the track and field star whose room was a few doors down. Jenner would win gold in the decathlon in Montreal, earning the distinction of the world's best athlete. In the cafeteria, Dad sat a few tables over from Olga Korbut, the Russian gymnast who was the darling of the 1972 games in Munich. In the dorms, he and his teammates watched on a TV monitor as Nadia Comăneci recorded the first perfect 10s in Olympic gymnastics history. Nadia was the talk of the Olympics. Montreal had made her a global superstar, but Dad felt no connection to the Romanian sensation. That era of his life was long behind him now. His teammates had no idea it had ever existed.

Dad couldn't help but pay special attention to the Israeli athletes in Montreal. They wore black ribbons on their outfits to commemorate those lost at the Olympics in Munich. In 1972, a Palestinian terrorist group had infiltrated the Olympic Village and taken 11 Israeli athletes hostage. All 11 were murdered. Known as Black September, the Palestinian group didn't act alone in their quest to kill Jews. They received logistical assistance from German neo-Nazis.

Before Montreal, critics doubted Team USA's construction. Pundits considered the team a long shot to win gold against seasoned European professionals. Robert Markus of the *Chicago Tribune* was succinct in his analysis of the roster: "A team of monkeys throwing darts at the entry list could have come up with a better group of players than the Olympic selection committee chose."

After the robbery of the USA's gold in Munich, the Montreal team was on a mission to reclaim America's basketball dominance. They may have been college kids, but each was determined to prove they were the world's best. The mission was personal for them.

Dad came off the bench during the Olympics. He'd averaged more than 25 points per game at Tennessee, but he was now a supporting player for Team USA. He was used to the ball going to him or Bernard down the stretch. In Montreal, it went to Adrian Dantley or Scott May — no questions asked. Thanks to Dean Smith's leadership, Dad and his teammates embraced their roles. They were focused on one thing: winning. Dad started games on the bench sitting next to Walter Davis, who would average 24 points per game as a rookie in the NBA a few years later. Dad was honored to have been selected to a team with such talent.

At Tennessee, Dad wore No. 22 after Dave DeBusschere. In Montreal, he wore No. 9, half of Judaism's special No. 18. The United States would go on to boycott the Olympics in 1980 in Moscow, so the next time a USA basketball player would wear No. 9 for the men's Olympic team was in 1984 in Los Angeles. That player starred for Dean Smith at North Carolina at the time. It was Michael Jordan.

At the Desmarteau Center in Montreal, a 4,500-seat arena built for the Olympics, Team USA recorded victories against Italy, Puerto Rico, Egypt, Yugoslavia, Czechoslovakia, and Canada. Dad fed the ball to Dantley and May and put his arms around teammates during huddles. Team USA's undefeated run through the competition set up a gold medal game against Yugoslavia, who had upset the Soviets in the medal round.

I have a picture of the moment the gold medal game ends. Dad can be seen running from the bench with a towel over his shoulder and both fists raised high above his head. He's a gold medalist at 21 years old. A faint mustache is sprouting above his lip. It's the precursor to the one he'd sport for decades. Dad's teammates are smiling and hugging near the paint area. Some of them are Black, some are white, some are middle class, and some are poor. They're from different states and have different religions. Together, they had become champions of the world. The scoreboard in the picture reads USA 95, Yugoslavia 84.

That score was bigger than basketball. It was more than a win over the rest of the world. It was a win over the idea that certain people aren't meant to do certain things because of who they are and where they come from. In the stands, Anyu and Apu were crying as the game ended. So were their friends, Joe and Helen. So was Dad's coach from Tennessee, Ray Mears. The other parents were crying, too. The Olympics represented a lifetime of dreams. For my grandparents, it felt like several lifetimes. They wondered what Lutzike would've thought about this.

When Dad stood on the podium and bent his head to have the gold medal placed around his neck, dressed in the stars and stripes, the Star-Spangled Banner echoing through the arena, Anyu was silent. The moment had been sent from heaven. She wasn't sure who'd sent it, but she had some ideas. After the game, when she finally got to see Dad, she threw her arms around him and asked how he was feeling. No one seemed to notice that she did so in Hungarian.

chapter 19

milk & honey

THE FIRST MACCABIAH GAMES, KNOWN AS THE JEWISH Olympics, were held in Palestine in 1932. It was the year the Nazis became the largest party in the German parliament. The next version of the games took place in Tel Aviv in 1935, with roughly 1,250 Jewish athletes from 28 countries making the trip to Israel. The Nazis were firmly in power in Germany by then. Recognizing that Israel was a safe haven for Jews, many of the participating athletes of the second Maccabiah Games chose to remain and settle permanently in Israel, an act known as making Aliyah. It would prove to be a life-saving decision. The entire Bulgarian delegation of 350 people made Aliyah after the games, including its wind orchestra, which had performed at the opening and closing ceremonies. It's like I always say: there's no wind orchestra like a Bulgarian wind orchestra.

In the aftermath of World War II, the Maccabiah Games have been held in Israel every four years in the summer after the Olympics. Jewish sports legends who've participated in the Maccabiah Games include Olympic gold medal swimmer Mark Spitz, Olympic gold medal gymnast Aly Raisman, Hall of Fame basketball player Dolph Schayes, U.S. Open champion golfer Corey Pavin, and my grandfather's training partner in Romania, Angelica Rozeanu, the greatest Ping-Pong player of all time. My dad is another Olympic gold medalist who competed in the Maccabiah Games.

When I landed at Ben Gurion International Airport for the 2009 Maccabiah Games, it was my first time in Israel. I'd just won a championship in Spain and had a year left on my contract playing in one of the top leagues in the world. Still, I knew that as a Jew, I could get an Israeli passport to count toward a local team's quota for home-grown players. That would make me more valuable on the Israeli market. I already had my Romanian citizenship, so a passport from Israel would complete a chain of documentation that would legally link me to my family's past. Dad too had held U.S., Romanian, and Israeli passports in his lifetime — just never at once. He renounced his Romanian citizenship when the family fled in 1964 and never used the Israeli passport issued by the government at that same time. After a decade with a green card in America, he received his U.S. passport to help the country win basketball games.

As I disembarked in Israel, stepping foot on its divine soil for the first time, I felt its warm sea winds wash over me. The summer air was hot and peaceful. The landscape was dotted with stone structures representing centuries of human history. Absorbing the energy of the Holy Land, the cradle of civilization, I realized that our two-week trip to Israel to participate in a sporting competition wasn't about sports or competition. It was about bringing Jews to Israel so they could know each other and the Jewish homeland. It was about connecting a Jewish diaspora that had scattered after the Holocaust with the only country in the world built to protect and preserve the Jewish people.

For the first week of the Maccabiah Games, our delegation toured the State of Israel, from the Golan Heights to the Old City of Jerusalem to the hills of Haifa. These were the cities where Jews found safety after the Holocaust. Most of my own family had settled in similar ones. Rubbing my hands against the grainy limestone bricks of the Western Wall, with Jews from around the world next to me pressing their palms and foreheads to the sacred structure, with some praying and some weeping, I began to feel Israel in my bones.

While traveling the countryside, always with a tour guide carrying a megaphone and a security guard carrying a machine gun, we heard stories of persecution against the Jewish people spanning millennia. This oppression framed our education of Israel's military might, helping us understand that compulsory military service for Israelis was an existential imperative. Threats surrounded Israel on all sides. When we ascended Masada, the ancient city on a plateau where Jewish soldiers committed mass suicide in 73 A.D. to prevent capture by the Romans, the sun in the distance was a blazing orange orb. It was too beautiful to be real. At Yad Vashem, the World Holocaust Remembrance Center in Jerusalem, I saw pictures of emaciated prisoners in Auschwitz and wondered if one could've been a family member. Floating in the Dead Sea, the lowest point on Earth, I felt like part of the land.

Once the basketball competition started, my Israeli cousins came to watch me play as they had for my dad 35 years prior. The gold medal game was held right outside of Tel Aviv. Our USA team found ourselves down three to Israel in the final seconds. Our coach, the great Bruce Pearl of Auburn University, had empowered me to lead the group. As our captain and top scorer, the responsibility to make something happen was mine. I wasn't someone who had the ability to create my own shot — I had to be opportunistic within the confines of the team offense — but I somehow wiggled free from my defender with a few seconds remaining and hit a floater in the lane, plus the foul. I made the free throw to send the game into overtime.

My mom, dad, and sister were in Israel to watch us beat the Israelis to win gold. I finished the game with 25 points and 12 rebounds. When the gold medal was placed around my neck, I was also handed the tournament MVP trophy. I took pictures with my family during the celebration. "At least one of us has a Maccabiah gold!" I joked with my dad, who'd won silver in Israel in 1973. I thought my Maccabiah gold medal looked like tinfoil Hanukkah gelt compared to his Olympic gold, but he didn't think that way.

"And an MVP trophy!" he replied with excitement. His pride made space for me to feel proud, too.

My sister later told me that my dad, while still sitting in the stands after the gold medal game, called my performance one of the best basketball moments he'd ever had. The athletic achievement ended up being a secondary benefit of the trip. The true value of playing in the Maccabiah Games was the realization that Israel is my home. Israel is home to every Jew in the world, whether they know it or not.

I boarded a plane weeks later for another country core to my family history: Romania. I was on my way to compete for the Romanian national basketball team. Again, the juxtaposition wasn't lost on me. My dad was born and raised in Communist Romania and won a gold medal in the Olympics for the United States. I was born and raised in an affluent suburb of New York City and would represent Romania in a low-level European competition.

Ultimately, I only lasted a week with the Romanian national team. There were five factors that impacted my decision to cut my time in Romania short. One, my teammates were smoking cigarettes butt naked in the locker room after practice. My usual post-practice routine consisted of a recovery shake and a deep stretch of the glutes and hammies. It's fair to say that I didn't feel perfectly aligned with my new team. Two, our starting center forgot to bring his shoes to the gym for one of our first games, and nobody seemed particularly bothered by that. On all the other teams I'd played on, shoes were prioritized as an essential piece of athletic equipment. Three, I didn't speak the language, and my teammates had no idea who I was. As an immigrant trying to make friends, there is incentive to overcome these types of differences. In my case, it was a battle I didn't have the motivation to fight. Four, there were horses in the streets pulling wooden carts of watermelons while stray dogs barked at them. These were scenes that would've made sense under communism, when my dad watched pigs get slaughtered in a courtyard, but they were hard to reconcile in the age of high technology. And five, my contract in Spain for the following season was the largest of my career and contingent on passing a physical upon arrival. Even a moderate injury in Romania would've jeopardized my season.

I left the Romanian team and never played for them again. It was the first time I'd quit something. It was a tough decision, but it was the right decision. Anyu had proven that she could fight through anything. Even she told me that sometimes it was healthy to give up.

A year later, after another season in Spain, I followed in the footsteps of my Jewish brethren from the Bulgarian wind section and made Aliyah to Israel. The citizenship process took about a month — far better than the 18 months I'd spent working to get my Romanian status.

I signed a one-year contract in Herzliya for $12,000 a month with the usual apartment and car provided by European teams. It was far less than what I'd made in Spain, but I needed a jumpstart, and Israel had been on my mind since the Maccabiah Games.

Once Sam and I got settled in Israel, the first question friends back in the States would ask was if we felt safe. I told them the truth: I felt safer in Israel than I did in the U.S. In Israel, malls and restaurants were guarded by security. Strict gun laws had basically eliminated unsanctioned firearms. Civilians in the street had all served in the military. From the minute Sam and I landed in the Jewish homeland, we were safe, secure, and at home. We spent our time sharing Shabbat with family and having lunches on the beach overlooking the sea. We'd eat dinner after games just outside the Old City of Jerusalem, a 15-minute drive from one of our apartments. When we'd observe the High Holidays, there were no explanations required for taking time off work.

On Friday afternoons after practice, Sam and I would visit our favorite street cart and top our falafel with massive piles of pickles, cabbage, garlic, hummus, and tahini. Sam showed restraint, but Anyu's cooking had conditioned me not to hold back. I'd stagger home from what we called "Falafel Fridays" in a comatose stupor to pass out on the couch for a three-hour nap. I'd wake up sluggish and sweating, reeking of garlic but feeling like happiness personified.

At sundown on Friday, Shabbat starts in Israel, and the whole country goes quiet as families gather for dinner. I'd occasionally spend Shabbat with cousins I'd never met who'd known my uncle in Romania. I'd always ask what he was like. They'd mention how handsome he was and how his little brother followed him every-where. I'd tell them my middle name was Leslie, after him. They'd shake their heads and say what a tragedy it was. Someone would change the subject.

I ended up playing for four years in Israel. The first and last were in Herzliya, a suburb of Tel Aviv. My middle two seasons were spent with the team in Jerusalem. For centuries, Jews had been end-ing Passover Seder with the wish: "Next year in Jerusalem." Adolf Eichmann had stood trial in Jerusalem for what he'd done during the Holocaust, with an emphasis on his actions in Budapest. Jerusalem is the holiest city in the world to the Jewish people. Coming from a family with a history like mine, it meant something to play basketball with "Jerusalem" across my chest. It was an important jersey to add to the family collection. It's nice to think that it might one day hang in a kid's bedroom between No. 18 Knicks and No. 9 USA.

A week into my fourth season in Israel, I knew it would be the last of my career. I'd groan as I bent over to tie my shoes before practice. I stopped getting to the gym early to work on my game and was quiet in the locker room. I lost the desire to meditate, something I'd done for years to stay centered while playing. None of that had happened before. I called my dad and told him I was done. The game had given me so much, I said, but I had nothing left to give back. The first thing he said was that few people could've overcome that knee injury like I had. Usually, he would've told me he was proud of me. This time he told me he respected me. That was better.

In the final weeks of my career, I was sick four separate times. I went straight from the hospital to the arena for one of my last games. When my coach tried to put me in, I was shoved into the narrow bathroom stall in the locker room having what I can respectfully describe as "a moment."

The stress of letting go of basketball was attacking me from the inside out, and my body was sounding an alarm. My only option was to put my head down and get through the season. Then I could start the next phase of my life.

My last basketball game was played at home against Hapoel Eilat, a team from Israel's southernmost city in the Negev Desert, right near Egypt, Jordan, and Saudi Arabia. We had to win the game to stay in Israel's top division. Being relegated to the second league would've been a disgrace for our club. I was the captain of the team, so the failure would've fallen on me. I couldn't imagine my basketball journey ending in shame. Actually, I could. I just had to hope the universe would let me walk away in one piece.

For my whole life, basketball had never allowed me to relax, so it was only right that my last game was decided in the final seconds. I'd started the game but had played just nine minutes. My only statistical contributions were three fouls; I had no points, assists, or rebounds. A broken-down veteran at 30 years old, I used to be a top performer in the league but was now relegated to the bench for the biggest possession of the year. I'd called my dad before the game just like I had every game I played in high school, in college, and as a pro.

Waiting for my career to end, my breathing felt constricted. I looked for Sam in the stands. When we made eye contact, she simulated a deep breath. It was the cue we'd established before the game to help calm me down. She mouthed the words: "It will be okay." I nodded my head and focused on the court. Sam was the only other person in the gym who knew I planned on retiring from basketball. I sat alone with the weight of this possession being the last of my career.

Our team was leading by one with a few seconds left. A made basket by Hapoel Eilat would end the adventure of a lifetime with a thud. The referee blew his whistle and prepared to hand the ball to the other team. I stood up and glanced at Sam again. She was looking right at me. My heart was raging. I'm sure hers was, too. With the crowd on its feet, our opponents threw the ball in, and the clock started ticking. One way or another, it would all be over soon. My teammates were flying around on defense, doing all they could to secure the win.

Despite being hectic and noisy, the gym felt still. The ball was in the hands of an old teammate of mine from Jerusalem. He was an Israeli national team player and a talented shot creator who now played for Eilat. He was the right type of guy to have the ball at a moment like this. As the seconds ticked away, he took several hard dribbles to his right and stopped on a dime, sending his defender off balance. Just before the horn sounded, he rose up for a mid-range jumper to win the game. I'd seen him make that shot hundreds of times during our practices in Jerusalem. I held my breath and tracked the shot's path. A jolt ran through my body as my career ended with the ball bouncing off the side of the rim. The noise from our crowd cracked like thunder. My teammates ran onto the floor and hugged one another. Our fans did the same. I put my hands on my head and started to cry. I walked over to Sam in the stands and buried my face in her shoulder. She was also crying.

It was April 23, 2014, almost 50 years to the day since my dad landed at JFK Airport as an immigrant in America. Basketball had helped him live an American Dream. The game had extended that dream to me. It was the vessel for my inheritance. When the last game of my career ended, Sam and I sat together in a quiet corner of the arena for more than an hour. I kept my uniform on and my shoes laced tight. I rested my mouth guard on my lap.

We reflected on all I'd been through with basketball. I told one story about rebounding for Michael Jordan and the Bulls at Madison Square Garden as a kid and another about a childhood friend thinking I was odd because I slept with a basketball. We talked about what it took to get to Stanford and what it felt like to play for the Knicks. From the time the photo was taken of me playing on the court with my dad at Knicks practice, basketball had rooted me in my relationships and provided goals to push toward. I'd no longer have the game in the physical sense, but its imprint would be permanent. I knew there'd be a mourning period, since it's never easy to let go of love. I also knew that the game would live inside me like the memory of a lost relative. It would survive through stories, histories, and silent recollections. A lesson, detail, or anecdote could always bring it back.

Contrary to what I thought as a kid, the game of basketball was never my end. It was a means to discover my end. Without the game, I could never have understood the depths of my family's past. Without basketball, I could never have connected with something that was so much bigger than myself. My playing journey was over, but basketball would continue to be that vehicle. I always felt that my career hadn't measured up to my dad's, but my dad himself once told me with tears in his eyes that he wished he'd been as successful as I'd been. It was easy to do one thing well, he said, but he was envious of how I'd excelled in different areas.

Anyu had never been able to pursue her education, he reminded me, but I'd taken our story down new paths. I'd graduated early and had been named an Academic All-American. I'd added new layers to our American Dream. Most importantly, he said that I'd treated people well along the way.

Basketball's real gift was teaching me that it's limiting to try to measure a life in points per game, grade point averages, or other arbitrary metrics of success. It's fine to strive for greatness, but as Anyu has demonstrated, it's far more lasting to take pride in your goodness.

When Sam and I finally got up from our seats after that final game, she walked me to the locker room and gave me a kiss before I entered. Everyone had already gone home. There were uniforms and towels all over the floor. The lockers were empty. The air was damp and steamy. It smelled like soap and sweat. My nostrils knew the scent well. I sat by my locker for several minutes, staring at the wall. On a few occasions, I just shook my head. I eventually took my uniform off for the last time. It slipped easily over my shoulders, as usual. I threw it onto the laundry pile and showered in silence. I knew Sam would be waiting for me when I finally emerged.

chapter 20

end & the association

O N JANUARY 30, 1977, TENNESSEE PLAYED UCLA AT the Omni in Atlanta. It was a Sunday. Tennessee was on top of the standings in the SEC and was the No. 7-ranked team in the country. UCLA was ranked No. 8, featuring star forwards Marques Johnson and David Greenwood. Dad was months away from being named SEC Player of the Year, an honor he'd share with his teammate and fellow New Yorker, Bernard King.

While Dad and Bernard dominated their competition, they couldn't escape the news of what was happening in their city. Those bred in Brooklyn, Queens, Manhattan, the Bronx, and Staten Island had a reputation of being fearless, so the constant fear felt by New Yorkers across the five boroughs had turned into a spectacle that was sweeping the nation. A serial killer known as the ".44-caliber killer" — soon to be assigned his lasting nickname "Son of Sam" — was terrorizing New York. He would kill six and wound seven in a spree of attacks in Brooklyn, Queens, and the Bronx. In a city of buzzing sidewalks and bustling subways, no one was safe. The killings prompted the biggest manhunt in the history of New York City. More than 20 years later, Spike Lee would make a feature Hollywood film to chronicle the phenomenon of Son of Sam.

At their temple in Queens, Anyu and Apu commiserated with other congregants about the killer. No one knew it yet, but Son of Sam could've been among them at temple. He was Jewish, and his next attack would hit close to home. In the early morning hours of January 30, the day of the Tennessee-UCLA game in Atlanta, the Son of Sam killer was less than a half mile away from Anyu and Apu's apartment. He was at the Long Island Rail Road Station in

Forest Hills, on 71st Avenue right near the West Side Tennis Club that hosted the U.S. Open. It was there that Son of Sam opened fire on a couple sitting in their car across from the Forest Hills station, killing the woman and injuring her male companion.

The victims who were shot in Forest Hills, while Anyu and Apu slept nearby, had come from the Continental Theater on Austin Street. They'd just seen *Rocky*, the Academy Award winner for best picture that year. The Continental Theater was the one that had charged my dad the adult price for his movie ticket when he arrived in America as an overgrown Romanian child, depriving him of snacks because he couldn't defend himself in English.

Son of Sam's name was David Berkowitz; he was a Jew from the Bronx. He was arrested outside his apartment in Yonkers in August of 1977 and sentenced to six consecutive life terms. He claimed to be following the orders of a demon that'd possessed his neighbor's dog. The dog was named Harvey. The neighbor was named Sam. On the day of the murder in Forest Hills, Dad was a universe away. Basketball had become an antidote that protected him from the hatred represented by events like the Holocaust and people like Son of Sam. He was an Olympic gold medalist and a college All-American now. He spoke English perfectly with no discernable accent other than that of someone from New York City.

Tennessee lost to UCLA 103-89 in front of more than 15,000 fans at the Omni in Atlanta. Dad had 23 points and Bernard had 31. They were both projected to be top picks in the 1977 NBA Draft. Basketball had only begun to change their lives.

In the 1970s, there was no real preparation for the NBA Draft. There were no trainers hired to address strength deficiencies. Players didn't travel around to visit teams or participate in group workouts organized by agents. A player's mom didn't require media training before the draft, and it didn't take a month to pick out the perfect outfit for the big day, knowing it would be televised around the world and it was one's obligation to look good.

After Dad's senior year at Tennessee, the only formal activities on his schedule were two All-Star games attended by NBA scouts. The East/West game was played in Tulsa, Oklahoma at Oral Roberts University. The Aloha Classic was held in Honolulu. Bobby Knight from Indiana coached in Tulsa, and C.M. Newton from Alabama coached in Hawaii.

Bobby Knight had led the Hoosiers to an undefeated championship season in 1976. Over his coaching career he pushed fans, was charged with hitting a police officer, threw a chair across the court during a game, head-butted one player and faced accusations of choking another. My dad found Bobby Knight to be funny and lighthearted in the low-stakes All-Star environment. Dad was named MVP of the East/West game.

C.M. Newton, Dad's coach in Hawaii, was from Rockwood, Tennessee and started his head coaching career at Transylvania University, a small liberal arts school in Kentucky. My dad was surely the only player Newton ever coached who was *actually* from Transylvania, the home of Vlad the Impaler, the birthplace of the legend of Dracula, and the resting place of Anyu's cherry trees. He won MVP at the Aloha Classic, too.

In addition to SEC Player of the Year, Dad finished his college career as the University of Tennessee's all-time leading scorer and the second top scorer in the history of the SEC, behind only "Pistol" Pete Maravich. He was already one of the most accomplished Jewish athletes of all time, and with his MVP performances, his NBA stock only kept rising.

Dad stayed at his parents' apartment in Forest Hills as he waited to hear where he'd start his professional basketball career. Son of Sam was still months away from capture, but Dad was too young and talented to feel vulnerable. He walked Queens Boulevard with friends, saw movies at the Continental, and played pickup basketball across New York, at Hickey Field in Long Island's Rockville Centre, at Lost Battalion Hall in nearby Rego Park, Queens, and at the Austin Street Playground right down the street in Forest Hills. He used to have to wait until it rained to get his own basket at the park. Now, whenever he walked past the fence, kids would clear the court out of respect.

Indications from his agent were that he'd be selected somewhere between eighth and 12th in the NBA Draft. Dad was keenly aware that the New York Knicks held the 10th pick. He couldn't think of anything better than starting his NBA career in New York City, with the team he'd grown up watching, just a cab ride away from his parents' apartment and Anyu's Hungarian food.

Before New York's selection, the Seattle SuperSonics had the eighth pick, and the Denver Nuggets had the ninth. Dad liked both cities and organizations, but they weren't New York. He'd prefer dropping a few spots if it meant coming home. The Boston Celtics had the 12th pick and had indicated they'd take Dad if he were still available. Red Auerbach was on record as liking Dad's heart and toughness. Boston was close to New York, and the Celtics were the league's most revered franchise, so it wouldn't be a bad outcome if the Knicks fell through.

It was the 11th pick that had Dad worried. He'd never been to Milwaukee before, but he couldn't understand why anyone would choose to live in Wisconsin. He knew they had a lot of beer, which was a plus, but he'd heard that deer roamed around as freely as people. He asked his agent if the deer stole food off the hot dog stands and was surprised to learn that — in a stark departure from the streets of New York City — there were no hot dog stands in Milwaukee. Romania was one thing. Wisconsin was another.

On the day of the NBA Draft — June 10, 1977 — Dad was at his parents' apartment in Queens. The draft wasn't televised, so he didn't know what time it started. At the moment he was selected, he was taking a nap on the pullout couch in the living room. It was the same one he'd shared with his brother before he died. Eventually, Dad was jolted awake by a ringing telephone. He was alone in the apartment, like he used to be as a kid. Anyu and Apu were at the store, as usual. It was a Friday, it was draft day, and it was also Anyu's 52nd birthday. Mostly, it was another day to work. They'd be home later. As my dad rolled over and answered the call, his huge feet hung off the end of the pullout. "Hello," Dad said, groggy.

"Congratulations!" his agent said.

"What happened?" Dad asked, sitting up. "The Knicks?" Dad held his breath.

"Almost," his agent said. "They took Ray Williams. You were next." Dad was silent. "You're officially an NBA player. Welcome to the Milwaukee Bucks!"

Dad needed a beer.

He learned that Bernard King had been picked seventh by the New Jersey Nets. He had a feeling six teams were going to regret that. Three of his Olympic teammates had also gone in the top 10, and another Olympian from Montreal was drafted despite not having played organized basketball since high school. In the seventh round, with the 139th pick, the Kansas City Kings picked Bruce Jenner, the gold medalist in the decathlon. Jenner was, according to Kansas City, the best athlete available. In reality, it was a publicity stunt. Jenner never played in the NBA. The draft was subsequently shortened to two rounds so only top players could be selected.

Dad called his parents at the store to tell them the news. Anyu couldn't believe a sport could do this much for a boy. Apu couldn't believe his son was going to make $100,000 a year in America. Dad couldn't believe he had to live in Wisconsin. I would later know how he felt.

As a rookie in Milwaukee, he averaged 6.9 points and 2.7 rebounds for the Bucks. In New Jersey, Bernard averaged 24.2 points and 9.5 rebounds for the Nets. Bernard was still a star, but Dad was now a role player.

Off the court, Dad enjoyed Milwaukee far more than he'd expected, like I would all those years later. In many ways it was like the Russian shtetl of Anatevka in the early 1900s, as portrayed in the zenith of Jewish storytelling, *Fiddler on the Roof*, one of Anyu's favorites. There were the obvious similarities between Milwaukee and the Russian village Sholem Aleichem had created: bone-crunching cold, liquid happiness guzzled nightly in dim bars, inordinate value placed on a healthy and productive cow.

More than anything, my dad lived his own *Fiddler on the Roof* story in Milwaukee because of the age-old tradition of Jewish matchmaking. My great-grandparents' marriage had been arranged that way — before Auschwitz. In *Fiddler on the Roof*, it was Yente the matchmaker that made the connections for the Jews in town. In Milwaukee, it was a Jewish family Dad had gotten to know upon arrival. The first question he asked over a big brisket welcome dinner was typical of a 22-year-old Jewish guy with traditional parents: "Any Jewish girls in town?"

The first name mentioned was Jerry Kahn's daughter, Nancy. It made sense. Jerry was one of the men responsible for bringing the Bucks franchise to Milwaukee. He'd helped land Lew Alcindor and Oscar Robertson and had been a part owner of the team all the way through the championship season in 1971. Judaism and basketball were once again working together in service of my family.

Jerry Kahn, who I'd call Papa Honey, was a founding partner of Godfrey & Kahn, one of Wisconsin's largest law firms. He was a pillar of Milwaukee's Jewish community, and since he also had a basketball background, my mom had grown up around the game. She could talk hoops and was more beautiful than any woman my dad had seen. She also had a special level of awareness and a keen intuition for the human experience. She could look into someone and understand what they contained. She read loss all over my dad's face and sensed the walls he'd built to protect his heart. She took on his complicated past, knowing they could have a future. My parents married a few years later.

For my Bar Mitzvah in 1997, Papa gave me his Bucks championship ring from 1971. It's 10-karat gold with a single diamond in the middle. *Kahn* is engraved on the side. Papa was raised poor and became a success through hard work and devotion to family. Over the years, he made regular donations to the Holocaust Museum in Washington, D.C. in Apu's name. A plaque hangs in the museum to this day with the name *Alex Grunfeld* on it dedicated by Jerry Kahn. When Anyu and I visited the museum together, we made sure to find it.

My sister was born soon after Dad was traded to the Kansas City Kings following his two seasons in Milwaukee. The year Becky was born, Dad was installed as the Kings' point guard after Kansas City's starter, Dad's Olympic teammate Phil Ford, needed surgery for an eye injury. Dad wasn't a natural fit, admitting in *Sports Illustrated* that he was "probably the slowest guy on the team." Sometimes, success hides in unlikely places. With Dad handling the playmaking duties, the Kings made it to the Western Conference Finals before losing to Moses Malone and the Houston Rockets in five games. In 15 total playoff games that year, Dad averaged 16.8 points, 5.9 assists, 4.2 rebounds, and two steals per game, the best run of his NBA career. At that time, Bernard King was bouncing from team to team. He'd been traded from New Jersey to the Utah Jazz and from

Utah to the Golden State Warriors. He was still a 20-point-per-game scorer, but he hadn't yet found the right home for his talent.

Meanwhile, Dave DeBusschere, the player Dad had modeled his game after, had become the general manager of the Knicks. After the 1982 season, DeBusschere made sure Dad's draft day disappointment was pleasure deferred, not pleasure denied. He signed Dad to a free-agent contract with the Knicks. Anyu and Apu had already moved to California, but Dad was now home — back among the cracked blacktops of New York City. He would live in the ritzy suburbs of New Jersey, not an immigrant neighborhood in Queens, but he would wear the iconic orange and blue of the Knicks, just like the players he'd watched from the nosebleeds with his father. It was all a dream.

He would come off the bench for the Knicks like he had most of his NBA career. Right before the season started, Dave DeBusschere found the player he would back up: Bernard King. The Knicks traded Michael Ray Richardson to Golden State for Bernard on October 22, 1982. Bernard immediately bought a house right up the street from my parents. Ernie and Bernie were reunited in New York City, but the show looked very different than it had in Knoxville. Bernard was an All-Star. Dad was his reserve.

My dad spent four years as a serviceable player for the Knicks. He played his last NBA game in 1986, nearly a decade after winning gold in Montreal and two decades after stumbling upon basketball at the park in Queens. His last game was appropriately in Milwaukee against the Bucks, where his NBA journey had started. My sister was five by then. I was two. The gym was packed for my last pro game in Israel, and there were roughly 1,000 people in attendance. The arena was only partially full for Dad's finale in Milwaukee, but there were still more than 11,000 fans in the stands. Dad had five points, three rebounds, three assists, two steals, and one block. His team lost by 38 points. He was 1-of-2 from three, making him 26-of-61 for the year. With that performance, he'd made himself eligible for the league leaderboard by attempting a minimum of 60 three-point shots for the season.

In NBA history books under league leaders in three-point field goal percentage for the 1985-86 NBA season, my dad is third at 42.6 percent, behind only Craig Hodges and Trent Tucker. Larry Bird made 21 more three-pointers than Dad attempted while leading his team to the NBA title that year. He also won the league MVP award. But he was fourth on the three-point field goal percentage list, one spot behind Dad. In '86, any victory over Bird was monumental.

Dad played a total of nine seasons in the NBA — two in Milwaukee, three in Kansas City, and four in New York. Anyu and Apu came to several games a year during his NBA career. Watching his familiar movements at Madison Square Garden, he was the same boy they'd seen bursting from his uniform that first time at his high school in Queens. The grown-up version just had more imposing shoulders and a mustache like Apu's. His teammates' eyebrows arched when they heard Dad talk to his parents after games. *What language was that?*

After the 1986 season, Dad had opportunities to continue his NBA career with the Utah Jazz or Cleveland Cavaliers. The Knicks offered him a job broadcasting games on the radio, with some college and pro scouting on the side. A yeshiva in Queens had once denied him admission for not speaking English. Now, he was being recruited to announce games on New York radio for the beloved Knicks. He took the job and hung up his sneakers, custom white Nikes with a big blue swoosh, his name etched on the side. They were nothing like the shoes he originally had in Romania, with their loose threads and thin soles, or the low-top Chuck Taylors that he paired with jeans and a T-shirt during his days at the park. When he got to college, he wore white converse piped with Volunteer orange to match his No. 22 Tennessee jersey, which was raised to the rafters in Knoxville in 2008. It's fitting that the final piece of footwear on his journey matched the orange and blue of his hometown Knicks, with his No. 18 jersey a clear ode to his heritage.

In the end, he had become a famous person in America, just like his brother had prophesized. Despite the dark shadows of the past, there had been a lot of love and a lot of basketball. That had been enough to get him through.

There are four major sports leagues in the United States — the NBA, the NFL, the NHL, and MLB. Of all the players who've played in all those leagues, my dad is believed to be the only one whose parents survived the Holocaust. Just because something's improbable doesn't mean it's impossible.

chapter 21

now & when

O NE DAY WHEN ANYU WAS 92 YEARS OLD, SAM AND I drove to her apartment for brunch. We'd been arguing with her for years by then, pleading with her, nearly begging her to stop making elaborate meals for us. They were still good enough to make me eat myself sick, but they took tremendous effort to prepare. We thought Anyu had earned the right to spend more time with her feet up and less time bent over a stove. We could eat something small and easy, we'd say. She'd never comply. "What are the chances she cooks something simple?" I asked Sam as our car rolled down a sunny California backstreet and approached Anyu's apartment.

"No chance," Sam said with a shake of her head. "No chance."

When we walked in, there were pots on the burners and plates covered in plastic, as usual. Swirls of flavor filled the apartment, but we couldn't tell what was inside the dishes. We had no idea how extravagant the meal was. After Anyu kissed us hello, she told me something unexpected. "Tatele," she said, "I decided not to make a big brunch for us."

I cut my eyes at Sam. She raised her eyebrows. Finally, progress. Anyu had listened. She'd taken it easy in the kitchen for once. "I made *ebéd* instead," Anyu said.

Sam and I again exchanged glances. My catalogue of Anyu's Hungarian food was always up to date, and I'd never heard of *ebéd* before. "Anyu, what's *ebéd*?" I asked.

"Tatele, you don't know *ebéd*?" she shot back, genuinely surprised.

"No, I don't," I said.

"Samike," she said, turning to Sam. "Do you know *ebéd*?"

"No, Anyu," Sam said. "I'm sorry to say I don't know *ebéd.*"

Anyu shook her head. "Neither of you know *ebéd?*"

"Hey, Anyu," I said. "Why don't you just tell us what *ebéd* is?"

Anyu smiled and nodded. "Of course, Tatele," she said. "*Ebéd* isn't a food. It's a meal. It's like a full dinner, only you eat it at lunch. I guess you could say it's a dinner at lunchtime."

Sam and I started laughing. Anyu's *ebéd* consisted of a soup course, a starter course, a main course, servings of fresh fruit after the meal, and an assortment of pastries she'd baked. It was a five-course dinner, eaten at 12:00 PM. It was *ebéd*, conjured in Anyu's sparkling mind, crafted by her wrinkled hands. Some things never change.

A year prior, at the urging of my parents, Anyu had left the apartment she'd lived in for 36 years to move into an over-65 community in the Bay Area. It was 25 minutes from me and Sam, but she didn't make the transition without a fight. She was adamant that she needed no assistance with her living situation. She was healthy and independent, well into her 90s but still walking a few miles a day; still driving with both feet; still winning local bridge tournaments; still drinking warm water, apple cider vinegar, and honey every morning to help with her arthritis, which hardly bothered her as a result; still making a living off the money she'd made at the fabric store, without needing anyone's help financially; still cooking enough *rántott hús* and *meggyleves* to get me violently ill; still doing all the dishes and scrubbing the sink after every meal — *ebéd* or otherwise.

In an ode to her favorite comedian, Buddy Hackett, she was still keeping rooms laughing with her jokes, including the gem I heard her tell at a holiday party about a paraplegic man ringing a woman's doorbell with his erection. She was still fasting on Yom Kippur, gladly refraining from food and water for 24 hours despite spending all day at temple; still remembering details of conversations she'd had 50 years earlier that no one else could recall; and still sharing with others what had happened to her family during the Holocaust and to her eldest son when they got to New York City, so their memories could live on.

It took a few months, but she now plays bridge five times a week. Her calm green eyes and neat white hair obscure the killer instinct lurking behind her smile. She still plays bridge to win, and she usually does. In the dining room, it takes several minutes to be seated with her because she stops and talks to someone at every table. She addresses the front desk staff by name and thanks them for their help. She has Wi-Fi and an iPad and learned how to videoconference with her family. When she cooks for us in her new kitchen, it's like she hasn't aged a day. Her steps are much slower than they were on the streets of Budapest, but they are taken with unmistakable grace. After sharing a meal with Anyu, a friend of mine described her as regal. He asked if she'd been a queen or monarch or some other type of royalty back in her home country. "Not exactly," I said.

When she and Apu still lived in Queens, in April of 1978, right at the end of my dad's rookie year in the NBA, the Bucks invited all of the players' families to Milwaukee to attend one of the season's final home games. The team booked flights and set aside two tickets for my grandparents. When Dad went to greet his parents before the game, he found Apu standing by the court, alone. He told my dad that Anyu would be okay, but she was in the hospital. She'd suffered a heart attack. It had happened a few days prior. Anyu wouldn't let Apu tell Dad over the phone. She didn't want him to be upset for his games. She told Apu to go to Milwaukee and share the news in person. She'd stay in the hospital and rest, and she'd be fine.

Anyu never went back to work after the heart attack. A few years later, my grandparents moved to the Bay Area to take advantage of the mild weather and slower pace of life. When I asked Anyu, a 95-year-old picture of strength and vitality who had outlived all her siblings by more than 30 years, how she could possibly have had a heart attack at 52, when she was still a young woman, she answered without pause. "Tatele, I lost my child," she said. "A heart cannot recover from that."

When I was born in 1984, Apu was battling liver issues originating from a likely undiagnosed case of Hepatitis acquired in the labor camp in Hungary. During one of Anyu and Apu's visits when I was a toddler, I waddled out of my room one morning and immediately asked, "How do you feel, Apu?" Anyu has always loved sharing how this innocent gesture from a child moved her dying husband to tears.

My grandfather passed away on June 9, 1986 from cirrhosis of the liver. It was a day before Anyu's birthday and a day before the anniversary of my dad's selection in the NBA Draft.

The night before Apu died, the Boston Celtics beat the Houston Rockets in Game 6 of the NBA Finals to win the championship. Larry Bird had 29 points and 12 rebounds and was named Finals MVP. Dad had played his last NBA game a month and a half earlier. Apu got to witness Dad's entire basketball career, starting with that first high school game in Queens.

Apu was born in Bala Mare, Romania, in Transylvania, but he received treatment as a dying man somewhere I would come to know well: Stanford Hospital. His funeral was at Schwartz Brothers Funeral Home on Queens Boulevard, the same place where my uncle's service had been held. Apu is buried next to my uncle at New Montefiore Cemetery on Long Island. Anyu has a plot reserved there, too. The stone is already placed. It's just waiting for her name and date. She's doing all she can to keep it waiting.

Anyu has worn her wedding ring every day since my grandpa passed away. She hasn't been involved with another man since his death. She says she had a husband and has never wanted another. After Apu died, she learned bridge, joined rummy games, and became more active at her temple. She paid for English lessons to smooth her accent and help communicate with non-Hungarian speakers. She talks often about the Holocaust, never forgoing an opportunity to share a lesson from her father. There are only a few surviving pictures of her parents. They hang in Anyu's bedroom.

On Holocaust Remembrance Day, Yom HaShoah, Anyu and I go to temple and listen to the rabbi read the names of the congregants' family members who were lost. Anyu squeezes my hand when she hears Solomon Samuel, Cecilia Samuel, Ernie Samuel, Margo Samuel, Eugene Samuel, Miki Samuel, and Heidi Samuel. She's encouraged me — that's not right — *implored* me to speak about the Holocaust. Her fear is that people will forget.

She was proud when the street outside the United States Holocaust Memorial Museum in Washington, D.C. was named Raoul Wallenberg Place. Wallenberg was a gentile who lost his life protecting Jews. He acted against injustice when it wasn't aimed at him. Anyu mentions Wallenberg regularly. She says there's no greater hero than him.

When I was getting my MBA at Stanford after my basketball career ended, someone spray-painted black swastikas all over campus. At the time, anti-Semitism and hate crimes were sharply on the rise in America. Not long after I graduated, a shooter stormed a synagogue in Pittsburgh with an assault rifle, shouting anti-Semitic slurs as he killed 11 Jews worshipping in peace. Hours before the attack, the killer posted a message on a social media platform. "HIAS likes to bring invaders in that kill our people," it read. "I'm going in."

HIAS, an acronym for Hebrew Immigrant Aid Society, is the same organization that brought my family spinach and an over-easy egg on their stopover in Serbia after they'd fled Romania. HIAS later helped my family come to America. Anyu couldn't sleep after the shooting in Pittsburgh, but she speaks clearly about America. "It's not perfect," she says, "but I wouldn't want to be anywhere else."

In 2013, ESPN made a 30 for 30 documentary film called *Bernie and Ernie*. It was watched by more than a million people when it premiered. Narrated by Chuck D from the rap group Public Enemy, the film was about a poor kid from Brooklyn, Bernard King, and an immigrant from Queens, my dad. They built lives and legacies, separately and together, through basketball. By the time the film was made, Bernard and Dad were in their late fifties. They rarely saw each other but talked on the phone every month or two. Whenever they connected, my dad would call just to tell me they'd spoken. Bernard is the only person Dad does that for. I can tell it makes his day.

Dad didn't want to do the ESPN documentary when it was initially pitched to him. He's private and cautious. His time running the Knicks taught him to be leery of the media. My sister and I convinced him to do the film. More accurately, we made him. *We're proud of your story*, we said. *Please tell it.* I only gave him one piece of advice leading up to the making of the movie: *talk about your brother.* I can count on one hand the number of times I've heard my dad bring up his brother. I know he thinks about him a lot.

As pictures of the two of them flash across the screen in *Bernie and Ernie*, Dad says: "My brother was nine years older than me. He was my hero. I followed him around everywhere he went. I wanted to be like him. About six months after we got to the United States, he developed some blood clots in his legs. He went to the hospital and it ended up being leukemia. In those days, there was really no cure for it. Unfortunately, he passed away a year later. It was hard. It was hard for me, obviously. It was very hard for my parents. He's always in our hearts and in our minds. It was a devastating loss for all of us at that time."

Dad's voice breaks slightly toward the end. He said all he could say. It was the most, by far, that I'd heard him speak on the subject. Anyu's apartment is filled with pictures of our family — we are her pride and joy — but there are no photos of my uncle on display. Even 50 years later, it's still too difficult.

Weeks before he died, my uncle's exact words were: "There's nothing I would love more than for my brother Ernie to become a famous person in America." My dad hadn't yet turned 10. He would go on to spend 42 straight seasons working in the NBA. He was inducted into the New York City Basketball Hall of Fame in 1994. He's the fifth-leading scorer in the history of the SEC. As an NBA executive, he was the general manager of the 1994 Knicks team that went to the NBA Finals. He overhauled the team, and the new version went to the NBA Finals in 1999. One of his Milwaukee Bucks teams made it to Game 7 of the Eastern Conference Finals. He built two different Washington Wizards teams that made it to the Eastern Conference Semifinals.

When fans and media criticized him, which was often, he kept his head down and kept working. He'd learned that type of focus from his parents. It's probably why he was one of the longest-tenured executives in NBA history. He was clear and succinct in the press conferences he did over the years. Only a handful of people knew that English was his second language and that he still spoke Hungarian daily when he made his regular call to Anyu. Kids in New York City had picked on him before he learned English, mocking him, laughing at him, and tricking him into crossing the street. Now, he can't walk down a street in New York City without someone yelling his name. In the end, he became a basketball legend and one of the most prominent Jewish athletes of all time. He fulfilled his brother's prophecy. His legacy is triumph. Because of him, so is mine.

One summer before my basketball career ended, Sam and I got married at the Corcoran Gallery of Art in Washington, D.C. The rabbi charmed the crowd as he described the great love Sam and I share. Standing under the chuppah, I raised my size-15 dress shoe and obliterated a glass as the crowd cheered *"Mazel Tov!"*

Sam was perfect, as usual, with her glowing green eyes and thousand-watt smile. After the ceremony, she gifted me custom Nike basketball sneakers in yellow and blue, our wedding colors, with "Groom" stitched on the side. She already had on her size-6 matching Nikes that said "Bride." We danced our asses off in those sneakers for the rest of the reception. My mom, dad, and sister danced alongside us. Anyu beamed, dressed in an elegant cream dress, her hair a wave of silver. Even Frank put on a blazer and left his fisherman's hat at home for the occasion.

I retired as a pro player in 2014 and didn't touch a basketball for a year. Still, I worked at the NBA and talked about the game with my dad every day. It's what we do. The game tortured me throughout my career, its significance weighing me down and its pressure wearing me out, but basketball is in my blood. Despite the tension, I've lived a happy life filled with wonderful people and incredible experiences. Basketball has been a huge part of that. I'll always love the game.

I'll love that basketball taught me how to work, how to sacrifice for what I want, and how to communicate and cooperate during good times and bad. I'll love that it taught me the joy of playing with different people from different backgrounds. That it taught me how to fail and how not to give up when it happens. I'll love that it helped me understand that your story belongs to you alone, and *that* in itself makes it important. I'll love that basketball gave me a way to honor those who came before me. That it gave me enough perspective to say that, if I could do it all over again, I'd try to enjoy it more.

Most of all, I'll love the memories with my dad. His gift changed the trajectory for generations of our family. When I see that ball, I know how much it's done for us. The bond that this game has created between me and my dad is eternal. The best thing about sports will always be enjoying them with people you care about.

Over the years, Sam has learned to cook Anyu's food. They've spent hours in the kitchen together going over recipes. They're the same ones my great-grandmother taught Anyu before the War. Anyu cooks with a pinch of this and a dash of that — never with measurements — but the proportions always seem to work. It's taken practice, but Sam has figured it out. These plates of food will endure. I'll be eating *rántott hús, piros krumpli, meggyleves, káposzta cosca,* and *almas pite* the rest of my life. Anyu calls Sam her granddaughter, and Sam calls Anyu her grandmother.

One Sunday in 2018, we had plans to spend the day with Anyu at her new apartment. Lunch was finishing on the stove when we walked in. I took in the familiar aroma of oil and breadcrumbs as I bent down to kiss Anyu. Sam and I suggested we relax for a few minutes. Sam and Anyu sat on the couch. I stood, facing them. I took out my phone to record. "Anyu," Sam said. "I have something to tell you."

"What, honey?" Anyu said, sounding alarmed.

Sam tried not to smile but was unsuccessful. "I'm pregnant," she said.

Anyu's posture straightened. "What?"

Sam's smile grew. "I'm pregnant!"

Anyu put her hands over her mouth. She knew we were undergoing fertility treatments and had spent a year and a half trying to get pregnant. After we found out we were expecting, one of the first conversations Sam and I had was about Anyu. We promised to teach our child what we'd learned from her. Treat people fairly. Be honest. Have the courage to stand up for what you believe in. Never stop fighting and never give up. Work hard. Love each other. Laugh a lot. I pray every day that Anyu will live forever, but even if she doesn't, I'll make sure her values do.

My legacy is complicated, but my obligation is simple.

Our son was born at Stanford Hospital on April 6, 2019. We gave him the Hebrew name of Lev, after my dad's brother. His first name is Solomon, after Anyu's father. Our son will know their stories. He will know all these stories. They are his now.

acknowledgments

T HIS BOOK WAS MADE POSSIBLE BY THE LOVE AND
support of countless wonderful people in my life. I've had
much good fortune over the years, but my greatest blessing is my
relationships. They are deep, strong, and lasting. I am so grateful for
that. It's an honor to be able to thank those who have been instru-
mental in helping me share this important family history.

I owe big thanks to my team at Octagon, led by my amazing
agent, Jennifer Keene. Jen never wavered in her belief in me, my
story, and my writing. She's a juggernaut, a confidante, a tireless
worker, a sounding board, and a friend. Thank you, Jen, for who
you are and for all you do. Thanks also to Alyssa Romano and Kayla
Wilkinson, a fun and fierce combination on the marketing side.
Thanks to Jeff Austin, a great source of friendship and support since
I was lacing up my sneakers as an Octagon basketball client. Thanks
to Chris Emens for helping me see the world.

Thanks to Josh Williams at Triumph Books for believing in the
promise of this story and for making very specific and enjoyable
references to college basketball players along the way. Thanks to
Jeff Fedotin for the sage editorial guidance and to Jen DePoorter
and Sam Frontera for the marketing firepower. Thanks to Noah
Amstadter for his oversight. The Triumph team is top notch and
was an absolute pleasure to work with.

It's impossible to convey the depth of my appreciation for my
friend Ray Allen. The world knows Ray's incredible basketball career
and undeniable cultural significance, but I wish his many fans had a
chance to know Ray as a man. He is an icon, but more importantly,
he is a mensch. His support for this project is one of the greatest

gestures of friendship and generosity I have ever experienced. The highest compliment I can give a person is to say that I'd want my kids to grow up to be like him or her. That is how I feel about Ray Allen. There is no doubt that we can all learn from Ray's example. Human beings don't come better.

In the earliest days of this project, I had several dear friends from Stanford who stood squarely by my side as I tried to make sense of a big and complicated story. Thanks to Glenn Kramon for sitting with me to work on this idea before I'd put a single word on the page. Glenn is one of the best professors I've had and one of the best people I know. Thanks to John Evans for letting me incubate this concept in his fantastic class, English 191. Thanks to Emily Peterson, my brilliant business school classmate who so generously gave feedback on the earliest version of this book. Thanks to the one-man powerhouse known as Cameron Lehman. Cam so adeptly coached me through the first telling of my family story and pushed me to peel back layers once I'd put it all into writing.

I'm grateful to the many historical sources that helped me contextualize my family's story, particularly those that chronicle the events of the Holocaust. I frequently referenced the United States Holocaust Memorial Museum's website, Yad Vashem's website, the Jewish Virtual Library, history.com, and many, many others.

Thanks to the sports historians who helped me understand my dad's place in Jewish sports history. Thanks to Major League Baseball's Official Historian, John Thorn, who I'm glad to call a friend as a result of this process. Thanks to hockey historian Dan Diamond and to Jewish sports historian Alan Freedman. I send a sincere thank you to my brothers at the NBA, John Hareas and Paul Hirschheimer. We've bonded over hoops history for many years, and I look forward to doing it for many more.

I did hundreds of hours of interviews for this book, and I'm grateful to all those who gave of their time and energy to help me uncover the truth of this story. Thanks to my grandma and dad for their tremendous love and patience as I consistently pressed on topics that weren't easy to talk about. Thanks to the late Tom Konchalski, our lifelong family friend, for providing precious details of my dad's early days as a ballplayer in New York City. Thanks to George Karpati for sharing his recollections of Budapest and Buddy Hackett. Thanks to my cousin Malka for the detailed account of what happened to her mom in Auschwitz. Thanks to all my other cousins and relatives who provided important details of what happened to our family during the War and beyond. A special thanks to Vera Spitz and Tom Szabo, both of whom helped me feel like I was spending an hour or two with my uncle. It's something I never got the chance to do here on Earth, but their stories of him and fondness for him made him come alive during our calls. Thanks for that, Vera and Tom. Thanks to the many others who shared tidbits, factoids, and anecdotes spanning decades, generations, and continents. This book became fuller and richer because of you.

Thanks to the many institutions that have supported me, including Nicolet High School, Stanford University, the Stanford Graduate School of Business, and the National Basketball Association. They have all left an extraordinary mark on my life. Thanks to all the people in basketball that I have called a coach, teammate, opponent, fan, or friend. I appreciate you all and am lucky to have been able to share such a great game with such great people. Thanks to Tomoo Yamada for all the work with my knee and thanks to Frank for being, well, Frank. There's only one of him, that's for sure. Thanks to Meredith Geisler for the many assists over the course of this project. Thanks to my awesome Stanford classmate Simone Burke for lending her smarts, experience, and creativity to help me think through a particularly important element of this book. Thanks to Tal Lee Anderman, my book coach, life coach, and Stanford sister, for always being there for me through this process and all the others.

I have friends in my life that I truly, truly love, and I want to thank them all. I have several best friends that I have called my best friends for more than 30 years. I am extraordinarily lucky to be able to say that. To my friends from New Jersey, my friends from Milwaukee, my friends from Stanford, my friends from the Bay Area, my friends who I played basketball with and against, I am grateful for you all. Thank you.

More than anything, this is a book about family, though it focuses on a specific slice of mine. There are people who I hold so close to my heart who are vastly underrepresented in this narrative. The first one I want to thank is my wife, Sam. I am reasonably sure that Sam is the perfect person, but I am *absolutely* sure that she is the perfect person for me. Sam is an immensely talented editor and thought partner, but she's an even better wife and mother. Sam is the definition of small but mighty. She helped me with every aspect of this book. She makes every day a joy. She is the best partner in the world.

Thanks to my mom, Nancy, who knows what I'm thinking and feeling long before I do. Not only did she make my existence possible, but she made my basketball career possible. She drove me to every game, supported me through every heartache, and cheered for me after every made basket. She is beautiful and accomplished and has a heart of gold. This book focuses on my relationship with my grandma and dad, but my mom's profound presence in my life could easily fill a book of its own.

Thanks to my sister, Becky, who has always been and will always be my best friend. Becky protected me when we were kids and has assumed the same responsibility now that we're adults.

Her contagious smile, warmth, and energy dazzle every room she walks into. And, it should be noted, her hair has never not looked good. More importantly, she is kindness personified. As Anyu says: "Rebecca does not have a bad bone in her body." It's the truth.

Thanks to my other family members who I love so much: Grammy, Lori, Cindy, Steve, Adam, Ruby. Thanks to the late Papa Honey, a titan of the Jewish community and an amazing grandpa. Thanks to Ryan, Ben, Sophie, Romy (The Queen), Abby, Dan, Miles, Caleb, and Rachel. Thanks to my in-laws, Doobah and Jim, and the other members of Sam's extended family with whom I've grown so close. Thanks to my cousins Fredy and Gabby. I hope I wrote about their dad, my great-uncle Andy, with the love and respect he deserves. Thanks to the many other cousins on both sides of our family who have shared this journey with me.

It is an indescribable gift to be able to thank my son, Solomon. He is a redheaded bundle of pure love, just like his mom. Solly is too young now to read this book, but he will one day know what it means to be proud of where he comes from. One thing is for sure: he makes his mom and dad proud every day. This all belongs to him now, as the last words of this book say. The legacy is in good hands.

Lastly, thanks to all those who have read this book. You made a decision to spend a significant amount of time with me and my family, and I am truly humbled by that. Thank you. There is a lot of pain and sadness in our history, but ultimately, this is a story of hope. It is my wish that this book will serve as a small reminder of the incredible power of hard work, perseverance, and love. Thanks to my dad and thanks to Anyu for teaching me those lessons.